Simplicity
FITTING BOOK

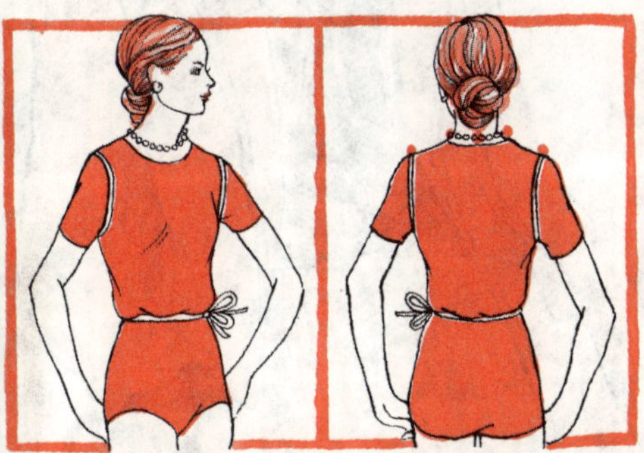

This how-to book tells you the ways to get the kind of perfect fit you've always wanted with a minimum of effort. Using any Simplicity pattern, or one of our Fuss-Free Fit® styles, try our streamlined approach to fitting. Just measure, compare and adjust . . . it's that easy!

Measuring Up .. pages 3-12
How to take measurements and choose the right size pattern for everyone you sew for. With handy fill-in charts you can keep your records up-to-date.

Fashion, Fit and Your Figure ... pages 13-16
Analyzing your own figure and applying today's fashion expertise to the clothes you sew is the key to a well-planned wardrobe with perfect fit.

Fuss-Free Fitting Handbook ..... pages 17-79
Starting on page 17, everything you need to know—fitting standards, all about equipment, pattern adjustments and fitting how-to's. Plus special sections on fitting pants and clothes for men and children.

Pro's Tips
Special advice from our experts—fitting secrets that help solve your sewing and fitting dilemmas are given throughout the book.

Managing Editor
Jo Kirshon

Project Editor
Irma Fischler

Art Direction
Consultants in Design:
John Barban, Jill Uss

Copy Editor
Alison Beyea

Contributing Editors
Janet DuBane
Susanna Pfeffer

Editorial Assistant
Andrea Bien

Illustrations
Sheila Camera
Durell Godfrey

ISBN #0-91-8178-11-8

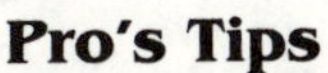

1

WHAT IS FUSS-FREE FITTING?

Fuss-Free Fitting is the best way to make clothes that look and fit just the way you want them to, with a minimum of effort.

Try to choose pattern styles that are flattering to you and require very little fitting at first. If you prefer more fitted styles, there are easy ways to fit those fashions that need special attention. This book shows you how to do it all, quickly and simply.

With our Fuss-Free methods, you'll learn how to fit the clothes you sew in three easy steps—

1. Taking personal measurements.

2. Comparing your measurements to the pattern body measurements.

3. Adjusting the pattern to your own measurements when necessary. Once you find the right pattern size, the rest follows easily.

Adjust the pattern before you cut into the fabric to minimize fitting problems. Follow steps one and two above. Knowing how to take your own measurements is all-important in determining your correct pattern size. Once your size is established, you'll be able to see exactly what adjustments

are needed. Many patterns won't have to be changed at all. Most people have only one, or, at the most, two fitting adjustments to make on a single pattern—in key areas like the waistline or hipline, for example.

In the Fitting Handbook, beginning on page 17, you can find your specific adjustments, the third step in Fuss-Free Fitting. If you do need to adjust your pattern, first try the Simple Pattern Adjustments that start on page 27. That may be all you have to do, with the exception of some very minor adjustments on the finished garment, such as raising or lowering a hemline. If you need to make further refinements, consult the Handbook for Special Pattern Adjustments, beginning on page 30, and make the changes needed to solve your particular problem.

Each Handbook page is keyed to a specific part of the body so you can easily find the section you want.

MEASURING UP . . .

Taking accurate measurements is the key to finding your figure type—determining the best pattern size for your figure—providing the right information about possible pattern adjustments—and in perfectly fitting garments.

On the next few pages, you'll find space to record all the measurements you take for yourself and everyone you sew for. Always write down each body measurement as you take it, and be sure to check measurements from time to time to record any differences—especially if you're sewing for fast-growing children.

Measuring carefully and accurately is the first and most important step in achieving Fuss-Free Fit. Follow these simple guidelines for the most professional results.

Measuring Guidelines

First, locate the major dividing lines and starting points of the body:

1. *The Waist*—tie a string snugly at the natural waistline (a).

2. *Base of Neck*—use a choker length chain or knot a long chain so that it outlines the bottom of the neck (a).

3. *Shoulder and Back Width Points*—place a rubber band around each arm so it rests at the end of the shoulder and forms a straight line down to the point where the arm joins the body (b).

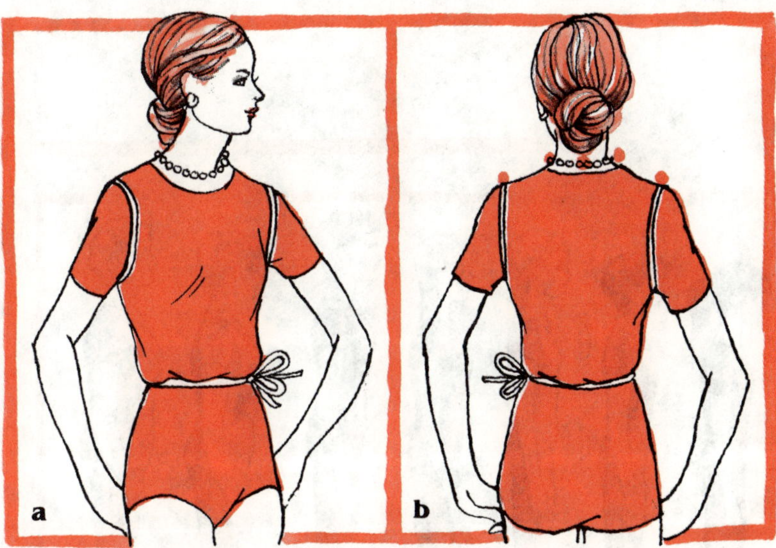

Mark two dots at the base of the neck, one in back at the first prominent neck vertebra and the other at the shoulder edge. Also dot the shoulder point (b). Then take the measurements you'll need to determine your correct pattern size. See pages 7–12 for how to's.

Some Measuring Pointers:

1. Always have a tape measure, string and a marking pen handy.

2. When being measured, stand normally, look straight ahead and wear the same undergarments and shoes that you'll be wearing with your finished garment—the undergarments you wear are important as they will contribute to the final fit.

3. For best results, hold the tape measure so that it is snug and lies smoothly, but does not indent the body. When measuring around the body, be sure to keep the tape parallel to the floor.

Sizing Up Your Figure Type

Once you've completed your measurements and written them down on the charts we've provided, you can select your figure type and pattern size.

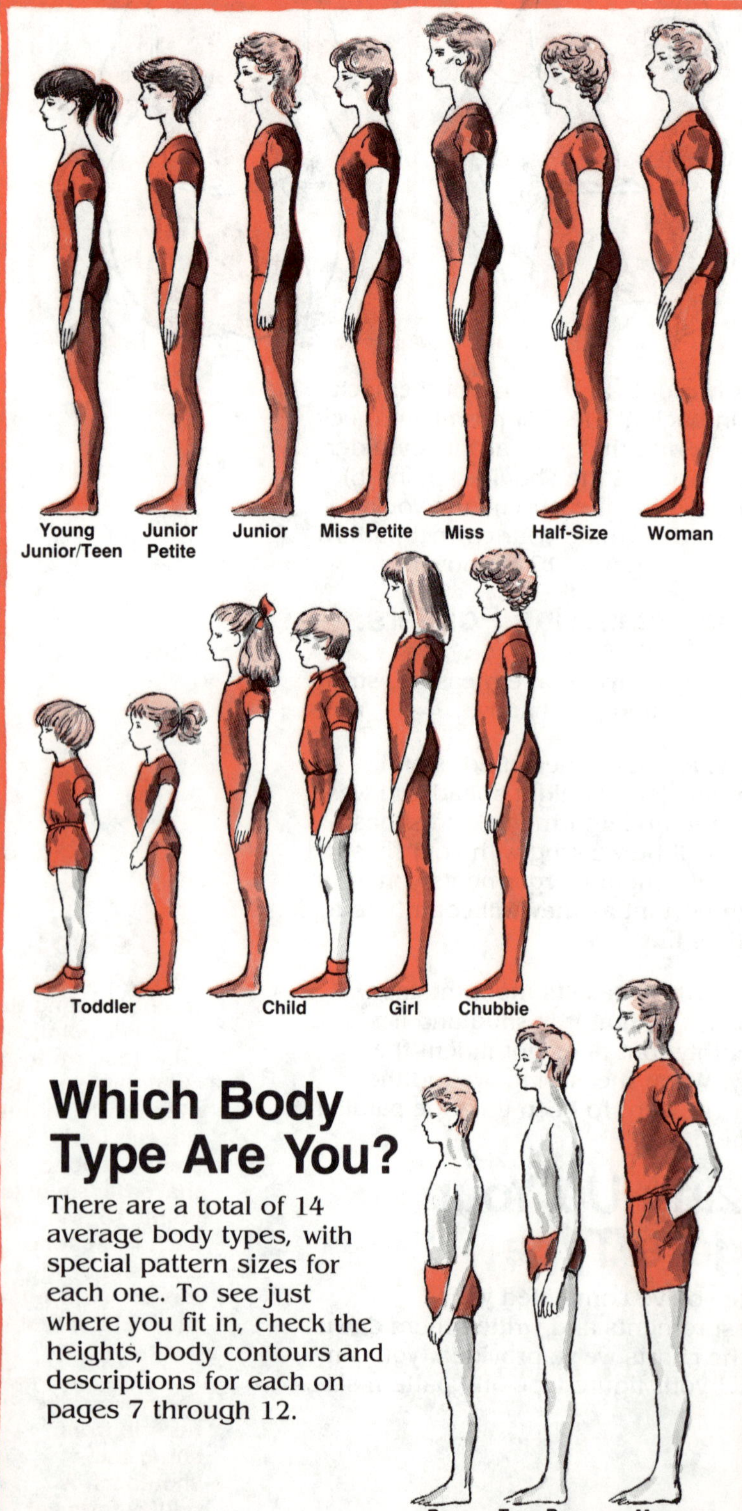

Which Body Type Are You?

There are a total of 14 average body types, with special pattern sizes for each one. To see just where you fit in, check the heights, body contours and descriptions for each on pages 7 through 12.

What's a Figure Type?

There are 14 figure types or size ranges in all—four for children, seven for females and three for males. Most of these are based on body types, with height and back waist lengths the most important for finding a figure type.

There are a few figure types that take age into account—Infants, Toddlers, Young Junior/Teen and Teen-Boys.

To choose your figure type, look at the figures opposite to get an idea of the different shapes, heights and body proportions. Read the short descriptions on the following pages to get a general idea of where you, or the person you are sewing for, fit in. Consult the body measurement charts on pages 7–12, paying very close attention to height and back waist length. Zero in on the figure type that is closest to your own. If you're in between, choose the one that's closest in back waist length.

Find Your Pattern Size

Compare your measurements on the chart you filled in with the ones for your figure type. The circumference measurements—bust or chest, waist and hips—are the keys here.

Most people's measurements do not match up exactly to any one size. If you fall between two sizes, select the smaller one. It's easier to add a little in strategic places and still achieve Fuss-Free Fit.

Some patterns today are made in multiple sizes with cutting lines for two, three or more sizes on each pattern piece. Look for these, as they will enable you to switch from one size to another on the same pattern.

All patterns include a certain amount of *wearing ease* or room for body movement. There is also *design ease*, determined by fashion shapes and silhouettes—like the ease allowed in a full gathered sleeve or a soft blouse (a). Extra ease is built into patterns for jackets and coats, designed to be worn over other garments.

FEMALES

Measuring and Sizing

Now you're ready to take your measurements. Look at the measurement guidelines and pointers on page 3. Then, fill in the chart on page 6. Be sure to take all the measurements specified on the chart.

These measurements are the key to fashions that really fit well. They'll also help you find your correct pattern size and let you know about any pattern adjustments you may need. Be sure to double-check your measurements from time to time and record any changes that might affect your fit.

Now you can select the right pattern size for each garment you plan to sew.

For dresses, blouses, jackets or multi-garment wardrobe patterns, choose size by *bust measurement.*

If your bust is 2″ (5 cm) or more larger than your high bust measurement, use the high bust measurement to determine your size for a dress, blouse or jacket that's fitted through the bodice. This measurement means that you have a large bust cup and may need to adjust the bust area only, rather than the rest of the garment.

For skirts, pants, shorts or culottes, choose your pattern by your *waist measurement*—it's far easier to adjust the hip area, and you won't have to alter the darts, pockets or any other waist details. An exception is for pull-on pants or skirts with elasticized waistline casings. In this case, choose a pattern by the hip measurement and then adjust the waistline. This assures you of a smooth fit across the hips.

Maternity fashions allow extra ease where you'll need it, so buy your usual pattern size. If you've just started sewing now that you're expecting, you can choose a regular pattern size by your *bust measurement* and figure type at first. But if you'd prefer your clothes to be large enough to fit for your entire pregnancy, then refer to the maternity charts on page 8.

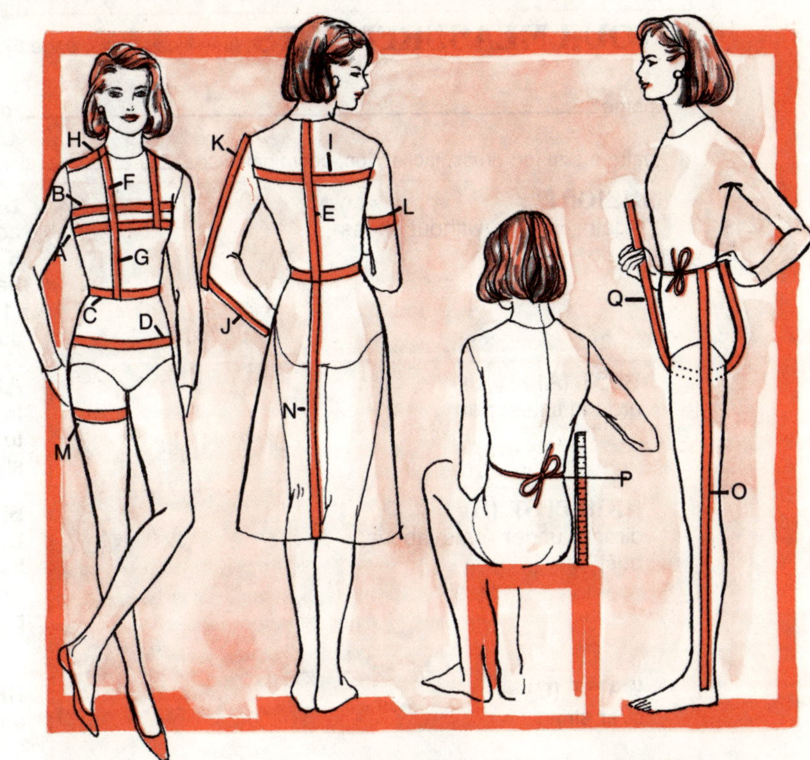

Bust (A)
High Bust (B)
Waist (C)
Hips (D)
Back Waist Length (E)
Shoulder To Bust (F)

Front Waist Length (G)
Shoulder Length (H)
Back Width (I)
Arm Length (J)
Shoulder To Elbow (K)
Upper Arm (L)

Thigh (M)
Back Skirt Length (N)
Pants Side Length (O)
Crotch Depth (P)
Crotch Length (Q)

YOUR MEASUREMENTS (see illustrations, page 5)

name ____ date ___________________________

pattern size for: dress, jacket, top, coordinates _______________ skirt, pants ___________ maternity ___________

HEIGHT against a wall, without shoes		**BACK WIDTH (I)** across back, 5″(12.5 cm) below base of neck or 4½″ (11.5 cm) on Young Junior/Teens	
BUST (A) around fullest part		**ARM LENGTH (J)** from shoulder point to wristbone, over slightly bent elbow	
HIGH BUST (B) directly under arms, above bust		**SHOULDER TO ELBOW (K)** from shoulder point to middle of slightly bent elbow	
WAIST (C) over string		**UPPER ARM (L)** around arm at fullest part between shoulder and elbow	
HIPS (D) around fullest part—9″ (23 cm) below waist on Misses, Women's, Juniors; 7″ (18 cm) below on others		**THIGH (M)** around upper leg at fullest part	
BACK WAIST LENGTH (E) from prominent bone at back neck to waist		**BACK SKIRT LENGTH (N)** from center back at waist to desired length	
SHOULDER TO BUST (F) from shoulder at base of neck to bust point		**PANTS SIDE LENGTH (O)** from waistline to desired length along outside of leg	
FRONT WAIST LENGTH (G) from shoulder over bust point to waist		**CROTCH DEPTH (P)** from side waist to chair (sit on a flat chair and use a ruler)	
SHOULDER LENGTH (H) from base of neck to shoulder point		**CROTCH LENGTH (Q)** from center back waistline between the legs to center front waistline	

FEMALES figure types and pattern body measurements

YOUNG JUNIOR/TEEN

The developing teen and pre-teen figure, about 5'1" to 5'3" (1.55 to 1.60 m) tall, with very small, high bust and larger waistline in proportion to bust.

INCHES						SIZE	CENTIMETERS					
5/6	7/8	9/10	11/12	13/14	15/16		5/6	7/8	9/10	11/12	13/14	15/16
28	29	30½	32	33½	35	Bust	71	74	78	81	85	89
22	23	24	25	26	27	Waist	56	58	61	64	66	69
31	32	33½	35	36½	38	Hip	79	81	85	89	93	97
13½	14	14½	15	15⅜	15¾	Back Waist Length	34.5	35.5	37	38	39	40
14⅞	15⅜	15⅞	16½	17	17½	Front Waist Length	37.8	39	40.3	42	43.3	44.5
8⅜	8¾	9⅛	9½	9⅞	10¼	Shoulder to Bust	21.3	22.3	23.3	24	25	26
4	4⅛	4¼	4⅜	4½	4⅝	Shoulder Length	10.3	10.5	10.7	11	11.5	11.7
12½	12¾	13⅛	13½	13⅞	14¼	Back Width	31.7	32.3	33.3	34.3	35.3	36
21⅜	21¾	22⅛	22½	22⅞	23¼	Arm Length	54.3	55.3	56.3	57	58	59
11⅞	12⅛	12⅜	12⅝	12⅞	13⅛	Shoulder to Elbow	30.3	30.7	31.3	32	32.7	33.3

JUNIOR PETITE

The short, well-developed figure about 5' to 5'1" (1.53 to 1.55 m) tall, with small body build and a shorter waist length than the Junior.

INCHES						SIZE	CENTIMETERS					
3jp	5jp	7jp	9jp	11jp	13jp		3jp	5jp	7jp	9jp	11jp	13jp
30	31	32	33	34	35	Bust	76	79	81	84	87	89
22	23	24	25	26	27	Waist	56	58	61	64	66	69
31	32	33	34	35	36	Hip	79	81	84	87	89	92
14	14¼	14½	14¾	15	15¼	Back Waist Length	35.5	36	37	37.5	38	39
15¼	15⅝	16	16⅜	16¾	17⅛	Front Waist Length	38.7	39.7	40.7	41.5	42.5	43.5
8¼	8½	8¾	9	9¼	9½	Shoulder to Bust	21	21.5	22.3	23	23.5	24
4¼	4⅜	4½	4⅝	4¾	4⅞	Shoulder Length	10.7	11	11.5	11.7	12	12.3
13¼	13½	13¾	14	14¼	14½	Back Width	33.5	34.3	35	35.5	36	36.7
20⅝	20⅞	21⅛	21⅜	21⅝	21⅞	Arm Length	52.3	53	53.5	54.3	55	55.5
12½	12⅝	12¾	12⅞	13	13⅛	Shoulder to Elbow	31.7	32	32.3	32.7	33	33.3

JUNIOR

A well-developed figure, slightly shorter than a Miss, about 5'4" to 5'5" (1.63 to 1.65 m) tall, with shorter waist length than the Miss.

INCHES						SIZE	CENTIMETERS					
5	7	9	11	13	15		5	7	9	11	13	15
30	31	32	33½	35	37	Bust	76	79	81	85	89	94
22½	23½	24½	25½	27	29	Waist	57	60	62	65	69	74
32	33	34	35½	37	39	Hip	81	84	87	90	94	99
15	15¼	15½	15¾	16	16¼	Back Waist Length	38	39	39.5	40	40.5	41.5
16	16⅜	16¾	17⅛	17½	17⅞	Front Waist Length	40.7	41.5	42.5	43.5	44.5	45.5
9½	9¾	10	10¼	10½	10¾	Shoulder to Bust	24	24.5	25.3	26	26.5	27.3
4½	4⅝	4¾	4⅞	5	5⅛	Shoulder Length	11.5	11.7	12	12.3	12.7	13
13⅜	13⅝	13⅞	14¼	14⅝	15⅛	Back Width	34	34.5	35.3	36	37	38.4
22	22¼	22½	22¾	23	23¼	Arm Length	56	56.5	57	57.7	58.3	59
13¼	13⅜	13½	13⅝	13¾	13⅞	Shoulder to Elbow	33.5	34	34.3	34.5	35	35.3

MISS PETITE

A short, well-proportioned and well-developed figure, about 5'2" to 5'4" (1.57 to 1.63 m) tall, with a shorter waist length and a slightly larger waist than the Miss.

INCHES						SIZE	CENTIMETERS					
6mp	8mp	10mp	12mp	14mp	16mp		6mp	8mp	10mp	12mp	14mp	16mp
30½	31½	32½	34	36	38	Bust	78	80	83	87	92	97
23½	24½	25½	27	28½	30½	Waist	60	62	65	69	73	78
32½	33½	34½	36	38	40	Hip	83	85	88	92	97	102
14½	14¾	15	15¼	15½	15¾	Back Waist Length	37	37.5	38	39	39.5	40
15¾	16⅛	16½	16⅞	17¼	17⅝	Front Waist Length	40	41	42	43	43.7	44.7
9⅛	9⅜	9⅝	9⅞	10⅛	10⅜	Shoulder to Bust	23.3	23.7	24.3	25	25.5	26.3
4⅝	4¾	4⅞	5	5⅛	5¼	Shoulder Length	11.7	12	12.3	12.7	13	13.3
13¾	14	14¼	14⅝	15⅛	15⅝	Back Waist	35	35.5	36	37	38.4	39.7
20½	20¾	21	21¼	21½	21¾	Arm Waist	52	52.7	53.3	54	54.5	55.3
12½	12⅝	12¾	12⅞	13	13⅛	Shoulder to Elbow	31.7	32	32.3	32.7	33	33.3

| | INCHES | | | | | | | | | CENTIMETERS | | | | | | | |

MISS

A figure that is well-proportioned and well-developed in all body areas. It is the tallest type, about 5′5″ to 5′6″ (1.65 to 1.68 m) tall, and could be considered the "average" figure.

INCHES

SIZE	6	8	10	12	14	16	18	20
Bust	30½	31½	32½	34	36	38	40	42
Waist	23	24	25	26½	28	30	32	34
Hip	32½	33½	34½	36	38	40	42	44
Back Waist Length	15½	15¾	16	16¼	16½	16¾	17	17¼
Front Waist Length	16⅝	17	17⅜	17¾	18⅛	18½	18⅞	19¼
Shoulder to Bust	9⅞	10⅛	10⅜	10⅝	10⅞	11⅛	11⅜	11⅝
Shoulder Length	4⅝	4¾	4⅞	5	5⅛	5¼	5⅜	5½
Back Width	13¾	14	14¼	14⅝	15⅛	15⅝	16⅛	16⅝
Arm Length	22¾	23	23¼	23½	23¾	24	24¼	24½
Shoulder to Elbow	13½	13⅝	13¾	13⅞	14	14⅛	14¼	14⅜

CENTIMETERS

SIZE	6	8	10	12	14	16	18	20
Bust	78	80	83	87	92	97	102	107
Waist	58	61	64	67	71	76	81	87
Hip	83	85	88	92	97	102	107	112
Back Waist Length	39.5	40	40.5	41.5	42	42.5	43	44
Front Waist Length	42.3	43.3	44	45	46	47	48	49
Shoulder to Bust	25	25.5	26.3	27	27.5	28.3	29	29.5
Shoulder Length	11.7	12	12.3	12.7	13	13.3	13.5	14
Back Width	35	35.5	36	37	38.4	39.7	41	42.3
Arm Length	57.7	58.3	59	59.7	60.3	61	61.5	62.3
Shoulder to Elbow	34.3	34.5	35	35.3	35.5	35.7	36	36.5

HALF-SIZE

A fully-developed, but shorter figure, about 5′2″ to 5′3″ (1.58 to 1.60 m) tall, with narrower shoulders than the Miss Petite and with waist larger in proportion to bust than the Woman.

INCHES

SIZE	10½	12½	14½	16½	18½	20½	22½	24½
Bust	33	35	37	39	41	43	45	47
Waist	27	29	31	33	35	37½	40	42½
Hip	35	37	39	41	43	45½	48	50½
Back Waist Length	15	15¼	15½	15¾	15⅞	16	16⅛	16¼
Front Waist Length	17	17⅜	17¾	18⅛	18⅜	18⅝	18⅞	19⅛
Shoulder to Bust	10½	10¾	11	11¼	11½	11¾	12	12¼
Shoulder Length	4½	4⅝	4¾	4⅞	5	5⅛	5¼	5⅜
Back Width	14½	15	15½	16	16½	17	17½	18
Arm Length	22¼	22½	22¾	23	23¼	23½	23¾	24
Shoulder to Elbow	14	14⅛	14¼	14⅜	14½	14⅝	14¾	14⅞

CENTIMETERS

SIZE	10½	12½	14½	16½	18½	20½	22½	24½
Bust	84	89	94	99	104	109	114	119
Waist	69	74	79	84	89	96	102	108
Hip	89	94	99	104	109	116	122	128
Back Waist Length	38	39	39.5	40	40.5	40.5	41	41.5
Front Waist Length	43.3	44	45	46	46.5	47.3	48	48.5
Shoulder to Bust	26.5	27.3	28	28.5	29.3	30	30.5	31
Shoulder Length	11.5	11.7	12	12.3	12.7	13	13.3	13.5
Back Width	36.7	38	39.3	40.7	42	43.3	44.5	45.7
Arm Length	56.5	57	57.7	58.3	59	59.7	60.3	61
Shoulder to Elbow	35.5	35.7	36	36.5	36.7	37	37.5	37.7

WOMAN

A larger, more fully mature figure, the same height as the Miss, about 5′5″ to 5′6″ (1.65 to 1.68 m) tall. All measurements are proportionately larger.

INCHES

SIZE	38	40	42	44	46	48	50	52
Bust	42	44	46	48	50	52	54	56
Waist	35	37	39	41½	44	46½	49	51½
Hip	44	46	48	50	52	54	56	58
Back Waist Length	17¼	17⅜	17½	17⅝	17¾	17⅞	18	18⅛
Front Waist Length	19⅝	19⅞	20⅛	20⅜	20⅝	20⅞	21⅛	21⅜
Shoulder to Bust	12	12¼	12½	12¾	13	13¼	13½	13¾
Shoulder Length	5	5	5⅛	5⅛	5¼	5¼	5⅜	5⅜
Back Width	16¼	16¾	17¼	17¾	18¼	18¾	19¼	19¾
Arm Length	23¾	24	24¼	24½	24¾	25	25¼	25½
Shoulder to Elbow	14⅜	14½	14⅝	14¾	14⅞	15	15⅛	15¼

CENTIMETERS

SIZE	38	40	42	44	46	48	50	52
Bust	107	112	117	122	127	132	137	142
Waist	89	94	99	105	112	118	124	131
Hip	112	117	122	127	132	137	142	147
Back Waist Length	44	44	44.5	45	45	45.5	46	46
Front Waist Length	50	50.5	51	51.7	52.3	53	53.5	54.3
Shoulder to Bust	30.5	31	31.7	32.3	33	33.5	34.3	35
Shoulder Length	12.7	12.7	13	13	13.3	13.3	13.5	13.5
Back Width	41.3	42.5	43.7	45	46.3	47.5	49	50.2
Arm Length	60.3	61	61.5	62.3	63	63.5	64	64.7
Shoulder to Elbow	36.5	36.7	37	37.5	37.7	38	38.4	38.7

MATERNITY

Maternity measurements are for a figure 5 months pregnant, and patterns provide ease to wear a garment through the ninth month.

INCHES

SIZE	6	8	10	12	14	16
Bust	34	35	36	37½	39½	41½
Waist	28½	29½	30½	32	33½	35½
Hip	35½	36½	37½	39	41	43
Back Waist Length	15½	15¾	16	16¼	16½	16¾
Front Waist Length	16⅝	17	17⅜	17¾	18⅛	18½
Shoulder to Bust	9⅞	10⅛	10⅜	10⅝	10⅞	11⅛
Shoulder Length	4⅝	4¾	4⅞	5	5⅛	5¼
Back Width	13¾	14	14¼	14⅝	15⅛	15⅝
Arm Length	22¾	23	23¼	23½	23¾	24
Shoulder to Elbow	13½	13⅝	13¾	13⅞	14	14⅛

CENTIMETERS

SIZE	6	8	10	12	14	16
Bust	87	89	92	95	100	105
Waist	72	75	77.5	81	85	90
Hip	90	93	95	99	104	109
Back Waist Length	39.5	40	40.5	41.5	42	42.5
Front Waist Length	42.3	43.3	44	45	46	47
Shoulder to Bust	25	25.5	26.3	27	27.5	28.3
Shoulder Length	11.7	12	12.3	12.7	13	13.3
Back Width	35.	35.5	36	37	38.4	39.7
Arm Length	57.7	58.3	59	59.7	60.3	61
Shoulder to Elbow	34.3	34.5	35	35.3	35.5	35.7

MALES measuring and sizing up

MEN'S MEASUREMENTS (see illustrations, page 10)

name ___________________________ date ___________

pattern size for: coat, jacket _________ pants _________ shirt ___________

HEIGHT against a wall, without shoes	
CHEST (A) around fullest part	
NECK (B) around neck at base	
NECKBAND* neck measurement plus ½″ (1.3 cm)	
WAIST (C) over string or waistband	
HIP† (Seat) (D) around fullest part	
BACK WAIST LENGTH (E) from promiment bone at back of neck to waist	
FRONT WAIST LENGTH (F) from shoulder at neck base to waist	
SHOULDER LENGTH (G) from base of neck to shoulder point	
BACK WIDTH†† (H)	
ARM LENGTH (I) from shoulder point to wristbone over slightly bent elbow	
SHIRT SLEEVE SIZE* from prominent bone at back of neck along shoulder, over bent elbow, down to wristbone	
UPPER ARM (J) around arm at fullest part between shoulder and elbow	
THIGH (K) around upper leg at fullest part	
CROTCH DEPTH (L) from side waist to chair (sit on a flat chair and use a ruler)	
CROTCH LENGTH (not shown) from center back waist between the legs to center front waist (see page 6)	
PANTS SIDE LENGTH (M) from side waist to desired pants length	

*a ready-to-wear measurement used for reference.

Be sure to read the general tips on measuring, pages 3-4, before filling in the chart. The measurements will help you choose the correct pattern size, and then decide what adjustments you need.

Take measurements over undergarments or a thin shirt. And remember, if you fall between two sizes, choose the smaller size to make your pattern adjustments easier.

For coats, jackets or jumpsuits, choose the pattern size closest to the *chest measurement.*

For pants or shorts, choose size by *waist measurement;* for shirts, by *neckband size* or by ready-made shirt size.

For wardrobe patterns with more than one item in the package choose pattern by *chest measurement.*

A special section on pattern adjustments and fitting for men begins on page 71.

Pro's tip:

Here's an easy way to take pants measurements. Use a pair that fits comfortably. Lay them on a flat surface and measure side length, crotch length and depth. On wovens, subtract 1½″ (3.8 cm) from crotch length and ½″ (1.3 cm) from crotch depth to get body measurements.

†usually 8″ (20.5 cm) below waist on Men
  7″ (18 cm) below on Teen-Boys
  6″ (15 cm) below on Boys

††6″ (15 cm) below base of neck on Men
  4½″ (11.5 cm) below on Teen-Boys
  4″ (10 cm) below on Boys

figure types and pattern body measurements

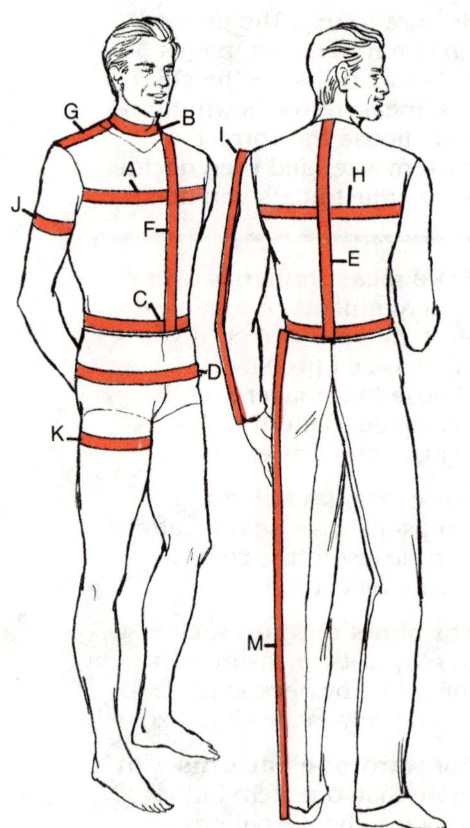

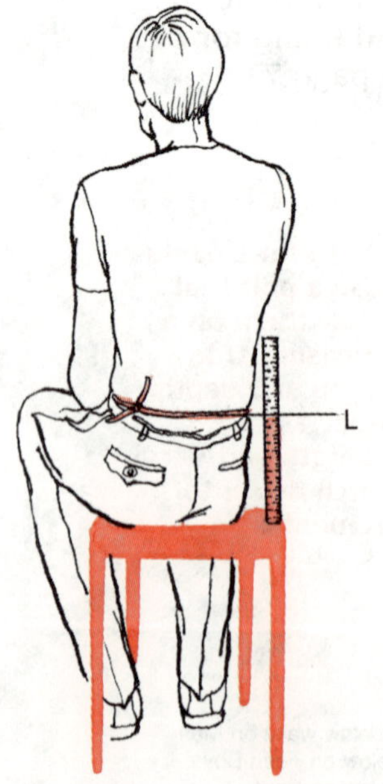

BOY

The just-developing figure, about 4' to 4' 10" (1.22 to 1.47 m) tall, that is starting to mature.

SIZE	INCHES 7	8	10	12	CENTIMETERS 7	8	10	12
Chest	26	27	28	30	66	69	71	76
Waist	23	24	25	26	58	61	64	66
Hip (Seat)	27	28	29½	31	69	71	75	79
Back Waist Length	11⅜	11¾	12½	13¼	29	30	31.7	33.5
Front Waist Length	12⅜	12¾	13½	14¼	31.3	32.3	34.3	36
Shoulder Length	4	4⅛	4¼	4½	10.3	10.5	10.7	11.5
Back Width	11½	11¾	12⅛	12¾	29.3	30	30.7	32.3
Arm Length	16⅝	17¼	18½	19¾	42.2	43.8	47	50.2
Neck	11¼	11½	12	12½	28.5	29.3	30.5	31.7
Neckband Size*	11¾	12	12½	13	30	31	32	33
Shirt Sleeve Size*	22⅜	23¼	25	26¾	57	59	64	68

TEEN-BOY

The young man figure that falls between Boys' and Men's sizes, about 5' 1" to 5' 8" (1.55 to 1.73 m) tall.

SIZE	INCHES 14	16	18	20	CENTIMETERS 14	16	18	20
Chest	32	33½	35	36½	81	85	89	93
Waist	27	28	29	30	69	71	74	76
Hip (Seat)	32½	34	35½	37	83	87	90	94
Back Waist Length	14	14¾	15½	16¼	35.5	37.5	39.3	41.3
Front Waist Length	14⅝	15⅜	16⅛	16⅞	37	39	41	43
Shoulder Length	4¾	5	5¼	5½	12	12.7	13.3	14
Back Width	13⅞	14½	15⅛	15¾	35.3	36.7	38.4	40
Arm Length	21⅞	22½	23⅛	23¾	55.5	57	58.7	60.3
Neck	13	13½	14	14½	33	34.3	35.5	36.7
Neckband Size*	13½	14	14½	15	34.5	35.5	37	38
Shirt Sleeve Size*	29	30	31	32	74	76	79	81

MAN

The man of average adult build, about 5'10" (1.78 m) tall.

INCHES

SIZE	34	36	38	40	42	44	46	48	50	52	54	56
Chest	34	36	38	40	42	44	46	48	50	52	54	56
Waist	28	30	32	34	36	39	42	44	46	48	50	52
Hip (Seat)	35	37	39	41	43	45	47	49	51	53	55	57
Back Waist Length	17½	17¾	18	18¼	18½	18¾	19	19¼	19½	19¾	20	20¼
Front Waist Length	17¾	18	18¼	18½	18¾	19	19¼	19½	19¾	20	20¼	20½
Shoulder Length	6⅛	6¼	6⅜	6½	6⅝	6¾	6⅞	7	7⅛	7¼	7⅜	7½
Back Width	16	16½	17	17½	18	18½	19	19½	20	20½	21	21½
Arm Length	23⅝	23⅞	24⅛	24⅜	24⅝	24⅞	25⅛	25⅜	25⅝	25⅞	26⅛	26⅜
Neck	13½	14	14½	15	15½	16	16½	17	17½	18	18½	19
Neckband Size*	14	14½	15	15½	16	16½	17	17½	18	18½	19	19½
Shirt Sleeve Size*	32	32	33	33	34	34	35	35	36	36	37	37

CENTIMETERS

SIZE	34	36	38	40	42	44	46	48	50	52	54	56
Chest	87	92	97	102	107	112	117	122	127	132	137	142
Waist	71	76	81	87	92	99	107	112	117	122	127	132
Hip (Seat)	89	94	99	104	109	114	119	124	129.5	134.5	139.5	145
Back Waist Length	44.5	45	45.7	46.3	47	47.5	48.3	49	49.5	50.3	50.7	51.3
Front Waist Length	45	45.7	46.3	47	47.5	48.3	49	49.5	50.3	50.7	51.3	52
Shoulder Length	15.5	15.7	16	16.5	16.7	17	17.5	17.7	18	18.5	18.7	19
Back Width	40.7	42	43.3	44.5	45.7	47	48.3	49.5	50.7	52	53.3	54.5
Arm Length	60	60.7	61.3	62	62.5	63.3	63.7	64.3	65	65.7	66.3	67
Neck	34.3	35.5	36.7	38	39.3	40.7	42	43.3	44.5	45.7	47	48.3
Neckband Size*	35.5	37	38	39.5	40.5	42	43	44.5	46	47	48	49.5
Shirt Sleeve Size*	81	81	84	84	87	87	89	89	91	91	94	94

*a ready-to-wear measurement used for reference.

CHILDREN'S MEASUREMENTS
(see illustrations, page 12)

name _________________________________ date _________

pattern size for: dress, jacket, top _________ skirt, pants _________

HEIGHT against a wall, without shoes	
CHEST (A) around fullest part	
WAIST (B) over string	
HIPS[†] (C) around fullest part	
BACK WAIST LENGTH (D) from prominent bone at back of neck to waist	
FRONT WAIST LENGTH (E) from shoulder at neck base over chest to waistline	
SHOULDER LENGTH (F) from base of neck to shoulder point	
BACK WIDTH[††] (G) across mid-back	
ARM LENGTH (H) from shoulder point to wristbone over slightly bent elbow	
SHOULDER TO ELBOW (I) from shoulder point to middle of slightly bent elbow	
UPPER ARM (J) around arm at fullest part between shoulder and elbow	
BACK SKIRT LENGTH (girls only) (K) from center back waist to desired length	
THIGH (L) around upper leg at fullest part	
CROTCH DEPTH (M) from side waist to chair (sit on a flat chair and use a ruler)	
CROTCH LENGTH (N) from center back waist- line to center front waistline between the legs	
PANTS SIDE LENGTH (O) from waistline to desired length along outside of leg	

[†] 3½" to 4½" (9 to 11.5 cm) below waist on Toddlers
4½" to 5⅝" (11.5 to 13.5 cm) below on Children
5½" to 7" (14 to 18 cm) below on Girls
6" (15 cm) below on Chubbies

[††] 2¾" (7 cm) below neck on Toddlers
3" (7.6 cm) below on Children
4" (10 cm) below on Girls
4½" (11.5 cm) below on Chubbies

Taking children's measurements requires a lot of patience and a little planning since you won't have their cooperation or attention for very long. Be thoroughly familiar with measuring techniques before you begin and choose your opportunity carefully. It's a good idea to check pages 3-4 to make sure you have everything you'll need before measuring children.

You might consider taking the child's measurements during a favorite TV program, or perhaps have something interesting for the child to look at—a colorful poster or picture, for example.

Fill in the chart as you go and be sure to include the date. If you're in doubt about the size, or if the child is between sizes, follow these rules: 1) *For Toddlers,* choose the size closest to the chest measurement. 2) *For all other sizes,* choose the size closest to the chest and back waist measurements. Since most children grow very fast, be sure to take a new set of measurements often (about every six months). This is the only way you can keep up with frequent size changes and avoid making clothes that start out too small. You can get ahead of children's growth changes by adding hidden growth allowances to their clothes.
See complete how-to's on page 79.

Pro's tip:

Can't find a child's waistline? Tie a string around the child's middle and have him or her bend sideways—the string will roll to the natural waistline.

figure types and pattern body measurements

TODDLER

The figure that is taller than a baby but shorter than a child. Toddler patterns have a diaper allowance and often apply to both boys and girls.

	INCHES						CENTIMETERS				
SIZE	1/2	1	2	3	4		1/2	1	2	3	4
Chest	19	20	21	22	23		48	51	53	56	58
Waist	19	19½	20	20½	21		48	50	51	52	53
Hip	20	21	22	23	24		50.7	53.3	56	58.3	61
Back Waist Length	7½	8	8½	9	9½		19	20.3	21.5	23	24
Front Waist Length	8⅜	8⅞	9⅜	9⅞	10⅜		21.3	22.5	23.7	25	26.3
Shoulder Length	2⅜	2½	2⅝	2¾	2⅞		6	6.3	6.5	7	7.3
Back Width	7¾	8	8¼	8½	8¾		19.7	20.3	21	21.5	22.3
Arm Length	10	10¾	11½	12¼	13		25.3	27.3	29.3	31	33
Shoulder to Elbow	6½	6⅞	7¼	7⅝	8		16.5	17.5	18.5	19.3	20.3
Approximate Height	28	31	34	37	40		71	79	87	94	102

CHILD

The child with the same chest and waist measurements as Toddler but taller, with wider shoulders and back. In many instances designs are suitable for both boys and girls.

	INCHES						CENTIMETERS					
SIZE	2	3	4	5	6	6x	2	3	4	5	6	6x
Chest	21	22	23	24	25	25½	53	56	58	61	64	65
Waist	20	20½	21	21½	22	22½	51	52	53	55	56	57
Hip	22	23	24	25	26	26½	56	58.3	61	64	66	67
Back Waist Length	8½	9	9½	10	10½	10¾	21.5	23	24	25.5	27	27.5
Front Waist Length	9⅜	9⅞	10⅜	10⅞	11⅜	11⅝	23.7	25	26.3	27.5	28.9	29.5
Shoulder Length	2⅞	3	3⅛	3¼	3⅜	3½	7.3	7.5	8	8.3	8.5	9
Back Width	9½	9¾	10	10¼	10½	10⅝	24	24.5	25.3	26	26.5	27
Arm Length	12¾	13½	14¼	15	15¾	16⅛	32.3	34.3	36	38	40	41
Shoulder to Elbow	7¾	8⅛	8⅝	9	9½	9⅞	19.7	20.7	22	23	24	25
Approximate Height	35	38	41	44	47	48	89	97	104	112	119	122

GIRL

The young figure, about 4'2" to 5'1" (1.27 to 1.55 m) tall, without bust development.

	INCHES						CENTIMETERS				
SIZE	7	8	10	12	14		7	8	10	12	14
Chest	26	27	28½	30	32		66	69	73	76	81
Waist	23	23½	24½	25½	26½		58	60	62	65	67
Hip	27	28	30	32	34		69	71	76	81	87
Back Waist Length	11½	12	12¾	13½	14¼		29.5	31	32.5	34.5	36
Front Waist Length	12⅜	13	13⅞	14¾	15⅝		31.3	33	35.3	37.5	39.7
Shoulder to Chest	6¾	6⅞	7¼	7⅝	8		17	17.5	18.5	19.3	20.3
Shoulder Length	3⅝	3¾	4	4¼	4⅜		9.3	9.5	10.3	10.7	11
Back Width	11¾	12	12½	13	13½		30	30.5	31.7	33	34.3
Arm Length	17⅞	18½	19¾	21	21½		45.4	47	50.3	53.3	54.6
Shoulder to Elbow	10⅝	11	11⅝	12¼	12⅜		27	28	29.5	31.1	31.4
Approximate Height	50	52	56	58½	61		127	132	142	149	155

CHUBBIE

The growing girl who weighs more than the average for her age and height.

	INCHES				CENTIMETERS			
SIZE	8½c	10½c	12½c	14½c	8½c	10½c	12½c	14½c
Chest	30	31½	33	34½	76	80	84	88
Waist	28	29	30	31	71	74	76	79
Hip	33	34½	36	37½	84	88	92	96
Back Waist Length	12½	13¼	14	14¾	32	34	35.5	37.5
Front Waist Length	13¼	14⅛	15	15⅞	33.5	35.7	38	40.3
Shoulder to Chest	7¼	7⅝	8	8⅜	18.5	19.3	20.3	21.3
Shoulder Length	4⅛	4⅜	4⅝	4⅞	10.5	11	11.7	12.3
Back Width	12½	13	13½	14	31.7	33	34.3	35.5
Arm Length	19⅞	20½	21¾	22⅜	50.5	52	55.2	56.8
Shoulder to Elbow	11⅛	11½	12⅛	12½	28.3	29.3	30.8	31.8
Approximate Height	53	56	58½	61	132	142	149	155

FASHION, FIT AND YOUR FIGURE

Fashion and fit may change, but basic figure types have a way of staying the same. Since today's clothes are not super-fitted, there are many easy-to-fit styles that not only flatter your figure, but keep pattern adjustments down to a minimum.

All About Fit

Fit has a totally different meaning today than it did a decade or two ago. Like modern lifestyles, today's fit is easy-going and casual. Clothes are less constructed than they used to be. Shapes are bigger, more relaxed, and although there is certain emphasis on

dressing up again, even these styles take on a softer, less fitted look.

Fashion offers many options to you. Of course, you can still choose *close fit* if you wish. Some closely fitted garments

like pants, for example, are shaped with darts or soft pleating at the waistline. Other choices include skirts that fit through the hips (a), some jackets, tops and shirts.

You may feel more comfortable with *semi-fit.* There are many styles that skim softly over the body, and do not define the shape underneath. A soft feminine blouse or a gently flared A-line skirt (b) are classic possibilities.

Then there is a whole range of clothes with *loose fit,* like oversized tops and full, gathered skirts (c). These styles all have one thing in common—they flow from the top. They must fit correctly at the shoulders or at the waistline, or the desired effect will be lost.

With all of today's options, but no really strict rules, everyone is free to choose the degree of fit that is right for her own shape and fashion preference.

Fitting Strategy

How much actual fitting will you need to do when you sew? With Fuss-Free Fitting methods, probably less than you think! Analyze your figure first: find your good points and the not-so-good ones. Then, learn to play fool-the-eye tactics by using the right degree of fit in strategic places and avoid unnecessary fitting problems. Consult the Guide to Fashion Fit chart on page 16. It will tell you just how much or how little fitting is required for many garment styles. When you're ready for more specific fitting how-to's, use the Fitting Handbook that starts on page 17 for step-by-step directions.

Be Figure Wise

Use fit to show off your good features and to play down your figure problems. Practicing this art of figure flattery can make all the difference in the way your clothes fit and look on you.

We'll show you how to select styles with the degree of fit that conceals your figure problems and enhances the good points of your figure.

How Do You Shape Up?

First, take a look at your figure and get to know your own good points and problem points. A full-length mirror is a must here. Wear your normal undergarments or leotards. Be sure to consider all the angles: face front, then sideways and check out your complete silhouette (a). Be honest with yourself; it will help you to avoid fitting problems later. Start out by classifying yourself in a general way. Are you tall, short, thin, top-heavy, or what? Then get down to specifics. Do you have square shoulders? Flat fanny? Slim waist? A too-large tummy?

In considering all these things, let your experiences with ready-made garments be a guide, too. If the same garment area seems to be a fitting problem time after time, you know that's a place to conceal by choosing camouflaging styles. Refer to the chart on page 16 for fashion help. Now write down your personal pluses and minuses. It's helpful to make two columns—one for the features you'd like to show off, and one for those you'd prefer to play down.

Conceal or Reveal

Let's talk about fit as it relates to body type. Your goal is usually to create the illusion of balance. Suppose that you are bottom-heavy, for example. If you make the area above your waist appear larger, the part below won't look so big by comparison. One way to do this is to wear something that is loosely fitted on top and semi-fitted on the bottom, like a big top over straight-legged pants (b).

Or perhaps you're the tall, thin type and would like to look a little rounder. Very close fit will only accentuate your bones and angles. So try wearing semi-fitted or more loosely fitted styles. A dress with a softly bloused bodice, full sleeves and a belt at the waist is a good choice (c). Always be sure the clothes fit well at the top—at the neckline and shoulders for a top, or at the waistline for a skirt—so they fall gracefully. It's important to keep an eye on hemlines. They are part of the fitting picture, too.

The right length can make the most eye-appealing proportions. With today's variety of skirt lengths to choose from, you should select the one that's right for you and the garment you are sewing.

Here are a few more suggestions that deal with figure problems and help you make the most of your own figure type through fashion and fit.

1. Shapely bustline? Closely fitted styles are your best bet—dart-fitted tops and jackets, princess lines, form-fitting knits that curve with you (d).

2. Large waist? Concentrate on loosely-fitted clothes that pass by the waistline. Hip-length jackets with just a hint of waistline shaping will give the illusion of a waistline (e).

3. Sloping shoulders? The use of shoulder pads can help balance the shoulder line in blouses, dresses and jackets. Set-in sleeves are preferable to dropped shoulder and raglan styles. Sleeves with puffed shapes, flange details help give the illusion of a broader shoulder line (f).

4. Trim, well proportioned hips? Wear close fitting fashions that show them off. Skirts with hip yokes, fitted pants (g), slinky knit dresses,—they are meant for you.

Now that you've got the idea, you can choose the kind of fit that will create the illusion that's right for you.

GUIDE TO FASHION FIT

You can choose to sew fashions that help you avoid unnecessary work. This guide gives you a general idea of which fashions require effortless fitting and those that need more. Once you have checked specific garments or details, below, you can tell by the pattern illustration which clothes are designed to fit casually and which have darts and seams that require fitting.

GARMENT OR DETAIL	LOOSE FIT	CLOSE FIT
Neckline	Gathered, bateau, slit necklines.	Jewel, crew, V-necklines. Scoop, square, sweetheart necklines.
Collar	Collars worn open or away from the neck. Notched, shawl, sailor. Bow tie, cowl or draped collars.	Collars designed to be buttoned. Band, turtleneck and shirt collars. Round, ruffled and cape collars.
Shoulder	Raglan, kimono, dropped shoulder or dropped armhole styles.	Set-in sleeves, sleeveless styles.
Sleeve	Gathered, puffed and other full sleeves. Shirt sleeves, capelet and ruffled sleeves.	Narrow sleeves in short, three-quarter or full lengths. Two-piece fitted sleeves.
Blouses, Shirts	Straight-hanging overblouses, smock styles. Blouson and full-cut styles.	Man-tailored shirts. Dart or ease-fitted princess or waistline-seam tops. Sweater or T-shirt tops.
Jacket, Vest	Unconstructed styles with minimal shaping. Cardigan and shirt jackets, windbreakers.	Jackets or vests with dart or seam shaping. Single and double-breasted blazers.
Dress	Slim or full without waistline seams, chemise, coat and shirt styles. Blouson dresses.	Slim or full styles with waistline seams and darts. Princess, A-line, sweater or T-shirt dresses.
Pants, Jumpsuit	Pull-on pants. Overalls and coveralls. Pants with wide legs.	Pleated trousers, dart-fitted pants with waistband and trouser fly. Jumpsuits.
Skirt	Flared, gored or gathered skirts. Bias cut, circle or wrap styles. Elastic or drawstring waistlines.	Straight or slightly flared skirts with waistbands, darted hiplines, pleats or yokes. Culottes.
Coats	Full styles, tied or wrapped. Capes, tents or duffle styles without waistline seams or darts.	Single or double-breasted coats with dart or seam shaping. Trench or flared coats; those with waistline seams.

What Fits You?

All of these fashions *can* fit you, but the ones on the left are definitely easier to sew because of their loose and unconstructed fit. The ones on the right are more fitted, closer to the body. They will require a little more effort to sew.

Fuss-Free Fitting

Fuss-Free Fitting begins once you have your measurements and your correct pattern size. The most important step is making the pattern fit. This will keep garment alterations to a minimum. The Fitting Handbook makes this very easy to do.

Get off to a good start by analyzing the elements of your pattern, following the fitting guidelines on pages 18-19. Learn how to judge good fit so that you can readily tell whether a garment needs fixing or not. You'll find out if your pattern needs adjusting, and get a general idea of what pattern adjustment and fitting are all about.

Everything you need to know for fitting a specific garment area—shoulders for example—is conveniently combined in one section of the Handbook, with the appropriate pattern adjustments and correct fitting methods. Most adjustments can be done right on the pattern, leaving only the fine tuning to be done on the final garment.

The handbook starts right at the top point of the garment, or shoulder line, and works down, exactly as you would do when adjusting a pattern or fitting a garment.

The fitting alert is a description and illustration of a specific fitting problem. These appear on the first page of each body section, from shoulders right down to derrière. Look for these alerts, as you'll quickly recognize your own fitting problems when you see them. Many of these can easily be fixed ahead of time right on the pattern itself.

Bonus sections of the handbook feature specific how-to's for fitting clothes for men and children, plus a special section on fitting pants.

The Handbook

WHAT IS GOOD FIT?

Our easy-to-follow fitting guidelines show you how to sew clothes that fit just the way you want them to. Illustrated here are the standards of good fit.

Use them as a guide when trying on any garment, and apply them to any garments you sew to achieve good standards of fit for all your clothes.

When checking fit, start at the top of the garment . . . at the shoulders and neck, or at the waistline for skirts and pants. The fit at these points affects

FITTING STANDARDS

Armhole seam is a smooth curve at the end of the shoulder. Sleeve cap has no puckers.

Jacket collar hugs back of neck. Lapels lie flat. Shirt collar has ½″ (1.3 cm) ease around neck.

Jacket tapers in slightly at the natural waistline.

Sleeve tapers from shoulder to wrist, hangs straight to elbow, then bends slightly toward front.

On man's jacket ½″ (1.3 cm) of the shirt cuff shows. Sleeves are long enough to cover wristbone when elbow is slightly bent.

Jacket hem is parallel to floor. Man's jacket covers seat.

Pants fit smoothly over hips and seat without wrinkling or bagging. Crotch is neither too short nor too long.

Center back vent on jacket lies smoothly over derrière, does not pull open (not shown).

Pants hem for man touches shoe in front; ends at top of heel in back. Woman's is about 1–2″ (2.5–5 cm) from floor, depending on heel height.

everything below. Garments that rest on the shoulders—shirts, jackets, dresses—must fit well at the shoulder and neck area in order to keep their style lines where they should be. A smooth overall appearance is your first fitting must.

Other key checkpoints are the dart positions, the armholes and seams. Horizontal seams should be exactly parallel to the floor; vertical seams should hang straight without swinging to the front or back.

Today's equipment can make fitting a lot easier. Here we've included the essentials as well as some extras that are especially nice to have, although they are not absolutely necessary.

The Essentials

Pencils and nylon-tip marking pen: For marking changes on the patterns that are easy to see.

Chalk or dressmaker's pencil: For marking fitting changes on garment.

Pins: Fine, rustproof ones are best. For easy visibility, try pins with bright-colored, round heads.

Transparent tape: To secure adjustments and repair patterns.

Paper: Tissue or brown wrapping paper is fine for pattern adjustments.

The Extras

Wrist pincushion: Puts pins at your fingertips when you're fitting a garment.

Seam ripper: A handy gadget for opening seams when you're fitting a garment.

Tissue tape and glue stick: Great for mending and adjusting patterns quickly.

Iron-on pattern cloth or interfacing: Makes it easy to try on a pattern for fitting; records adjustments, too.

Yardstick (or meter stick): For measuring yardage, checking grainlines.

Tape measure: For taking body and pattern measurements.

Scissors: Fabric, sewing, and paper scissors are handy for making pattern adjustments.

See-through rulers: In various sizes and shapes; a must for pattern adjustments and markings.

French curves: Use to redraw armholes, necklines and other curves for pattern adjustments.

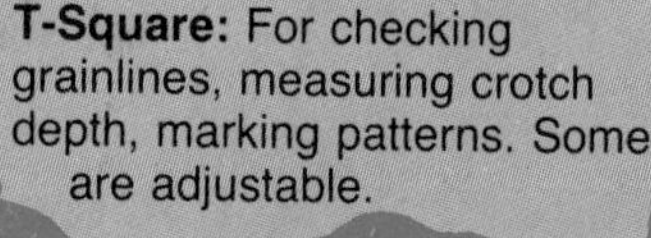

T-Square: For checking grainlines, measuring crotch depth, marking patterns. Some are adjustable.

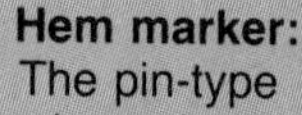

Hem marker: The pin-type shown here marks accurately; requires a helper.

MAKING THE PATTERN FIT YOU

Whether you have to adjust your pattern or not depends on two things—your own measurements—and the degree of fit you prefer. Some patterns won't need any adjustments; others only one or two to make the fashion look and feel right. Consult the Fuss-Free Fashion Guide on page 16. That will give you an idea of how much fitting you may have to do. Then, use the following pages to find out what changes, if any, are needed.

The most exact method of finding out if a pattern will fit you is to compare your own body measurements to the pattern body measurements, using the chart on page 22. This will provide valuable information about how many pattern adjustments you'll have to make.

All about ease

Before you make your comparison between your measurements and those of the pattern, it's important to know about ease. Whatever degree of fit you prefer—tight, semi-fit or loose—all have something essential in common—ease. Ease is that extra fullness that lets you move around comfortably. This is why the actual pattern measures more than the pattern body measurements (a).

The amount of ease allowed by a fashion designer determines the silhouette and the way the garment is intended to fit. Just about every fashion, with the exception of swimwear, has some ease built into its design.

The chart on page 22 lists minimum wearing ease for today's fitting standards. Most contemporary styles come with even more ease or design fullness. It's advisable not to go below the minimum ease when adjusting your pattern. Once you've been sewing a while, you may decide that you prefer a tighter or looser fit than the pattern design allows. Then you can make the necessary adjustments to suit you.

PATTERN ADJUSTMENT CHART

	BODY MEASUREMENTS		Adjustments
	Yours	**Pattern**	**(+ or −)**
Length & Width:		(see pages 7-12)	
1. Front Waist Length	______	______	______
2. Shoulder to Bust	______	______	______
3. Back Waist Length	______	______	______
4. Shoulder Length	______	______	______
5. Back Width	______	______	______
6. Arm Length	______	______	______
7. Shoulder to Elbow (females only)	______	______	______
Circumference:	**Minimum Ease For Wovens***	**Ease Allowed**	
8. Bust/Chest	______ 2″ (5 cm)	______	______
9. Waist	______ ½″ (1.3 cm)	______	______
10. Hips	______ 2″ (5 cm)	______	______
11. Upper Arm (for sleeve width)	______ 2-2½″ (5-6.3 cm)	** ______	______
12. Neck (males only)	______ ½″ (1.3 cm)	______	______
	GARMENT MEASUREMENT		
Finished Length:			
13. Back Skirt Length	______	______ (see envelope back)	

*For stretchy knits, do not allow as much ease.   ** Measure pattern and subtract 2-2½″ (5-6.3 cm) for plain sleeves.

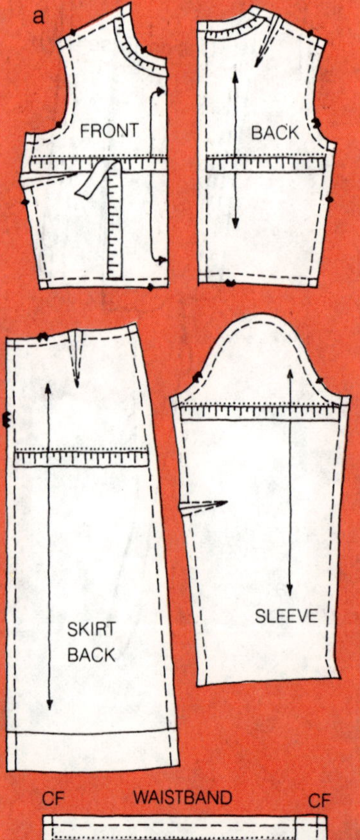

Compare your body measurements to the pattern body measurements. You'll see how much to adjust. Write your measurements on the chart, then those for the pattern body, using the information on pages 7-12). Compare these columns; fill in any differences (+ or −).

For length and width, adjust the pattern if there is any difference at all.

For circumference, adjust if the difference is more than 1″ (2.5 cm). If it is less, you may not have to adjust 8-12 on the chart. This system maintains the ease intended by the designer. For pants, see page 63.

A note about design ease: Comparing the ease allowed in the pattern to the minimum ease (wearing ease) will tell you how much design fullness the pattern has. To see how much ease there is, subtract the pattern body from the actual pattern measurements at points 8–12. Measure from seamline to seamline (a) and total the front and back. Simplicity Fuss-Free

Fit® patterns have printed guidelines to show you exactly where to measure and adjust, other Simplicity patterns do not. However, you can draw lines on these patterns as follows:

To locate the bustline, subtract #2 from #1 on the chart above and measure up that distance from the waistline mark. For sleeve width (upper arm) and hip, measure at fullest part (check measurement charts, pages 6-12). Measure neck on collar, and waist on waistband piece, from closure centers, rather than the seamlines. If there is no collar or waistband, stand the tape on edge and measure from centers. Do not include darts.

The only exceptions to the ease listed are garments like strapless gowns, those worn over other garments and those designed for stretchable knits. Knits that "give" require little or no ease in the pattern.

ADJUSTMENT GROUND RULES

Make length (except finished side or back length) and width changes first, then adjust for circumference. Make any other special adjustments working from the top of the pattern downward. As your last step, double-check overall lengths.

If you make an adjustment on one pattern piece, you may have to make a corresponding change on a piece that will be stitched to that one. For example, if you lengthen the bodice front, you'll have to do the same on the back and on any facings. If you change a neckline, make the same change on the facing or the collar pattern piece (b).

To correct a straight cutting line that's been thrown off-course by an adjustment, use a ruler to draw the new line, tapering it gradually to the old one (c). Redraw curved lines freehand or with a French curve; use the part of the curve that matches the original line (d).

Once all adjustments have been made, double-check to see that corrected seamlines on fronts and backs match up, and that they are corrected along the cutting lines. Check to see that symbols or notches match and that pattern lies perfectly flat.

Now, adjust the pattern

Since some adjustments can distort others, follow the numbered chart on page 22.

1. **Make length and width adjustments.** Make these changes in all areas from 1 to 7 on the chart where they are needed. See page 27 for specific how-to's.

2. **Make circumference adjustments.** Begin by marking any changes needed for 8-12 on the chart, at the side seamlines. Redraw the seamlines and cutting lines at the marks, as shown on pages 28-29.

3. **Make any special adjustments.** Because these should also be done in the right sequence to avoid one adjustment from throwing off another, the Fitting Handbook is arranged in the order that adjustments should be made:

Shoulders	Armhole
Neck	Sleeve
Chest	Abdomen
Bust	Hips
Back	Derrière

Read the general fitting tips next. Then, if you suspect problems in any of the above areas, go directly to that section in Special Pattern Adjustments. Remember that you probably won't have to make more than one or two major adjustments in a single pattern.

4. **Adjust side or back lengths.** See the section on hems on page 27.

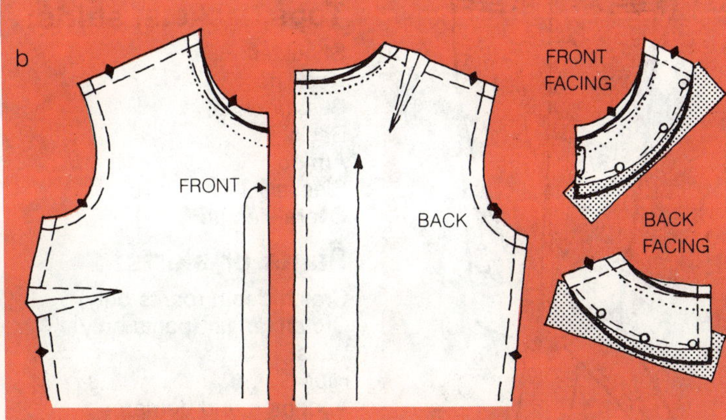

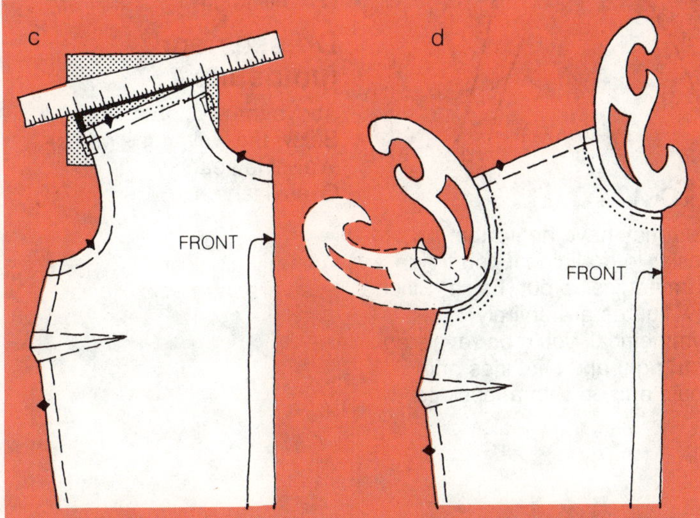

FITTING METHODS
Guidelines for achieving better fit as you sew

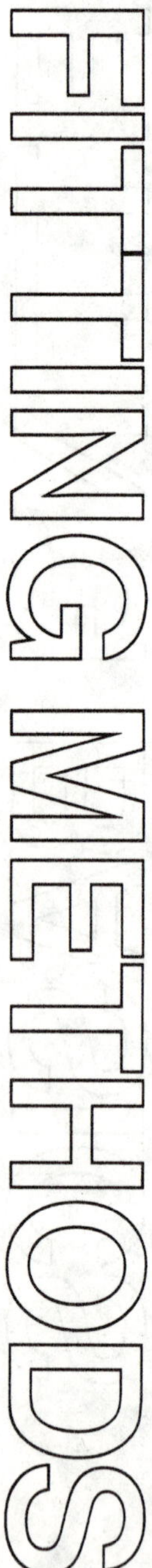

When to Fit

Checking the fit of the garment early in the sewing process accomplishes two things—it lets you see how the garment is going to look, and allows you to make any necessary fitting adjustments.

When to check? As soon as any darts are stitched and the shoulder and side seams pinned or basted (a). If you're making a skirt or pants, check fit after you've stitched darts, pinned or basted side seams and crotch seams (pants and culottes only), and basted the waistband in place. You can final-stitch these seams if you are sure the garment will fit.

Postpone applying zippers, sleeves, facings, collars and pockets. If you are lining the garment, try it on with the lining pinned to the inside.

Essential check points

Check the garment for overall appearance. Is it symmetrical? Are the seams and grainlines straight? Check the shoulders and the neckline. Do they fit well? Are there wrinkles that indicate strain? If there are darts, are they in the right position? Are there folds in the garment that indicate too much fullness? After you've checked and marked whatever adjustments you need, you can final stitch and press the seams, set in the sleeves and check other details.

You can have your final try-on fitting session when the garment is ready for the hem, any buttonholes, trims or pockets. This is a good time to check for any additional minor changes. Check the position of applied pockets, belts, tabs or flaps and any trims. Hold them up or pin them to the garment to see where they look best if you are changing them from the pattern positioning. Then mark their positions with pins or tailor's chalk (a).

When you're satisfied with the fit of your garment and all its details, mark the hem; finish the garment.

How to fit

You may have heard that it's easier to do fitting if you try on a garment inside out. False! Since few figures are entirely symmetrical, you'd be reversing your right and left sides and could end up with a lopsided garment. Do all your fitting with the garment right side out. It's very simple to transfer your changes to the wrong side for stitching later.

When you are fitting make sure to wear the same undergarments and shoes you plan to wear with the finished garment.

Fit with a relaxed feeling. In other words, don't fit too closely for your figure. A trim fit is flattering to a slim figure, but a looser fit is kinder to a large one.

Always start at the top of the garment and work down. Very often a slight change in the fit of the shoulders or neckline can improve the fit of the entire garment. Make fitting changes in the order listed below, checking the total appearance of your garment after each change.

Tops, jackets, shirts:

Shoulder
Neckline
Bust or chest
Back
Armhole
Sleeve
Overall length

Pants or skirts:

Crotch depth (pants only)
Crotch length (pants only)
Waist
Hips
Abdomen and derrière
Crotch smile or droop (pants)
Overall length

Dresses and jumpsuits

Above the waist (see tops)
Below the waist (see pants)
Waistline seam
Overall length

Changing seams: Watch for wrinkles and folds as you fit. They are clues to areas that need adjustment.

If the garment area is too tight, wrinkles or pulls will point to the area where there is stress (b). When this occurs, open the side seams to relieve the strain and let out the seam, up to ⅜″ (1 cm) for each seam allowance. Then pin a new seamline (c).

If the garment area is too loose, folds will form parallel to the seams that need to be taken in. If the folds fall vertically (d), smooth out the excess fabric to the side seams and pin. Mark the new seamlines (e).

When the folds fall horizontally on the garment (f), you can open the seam and smooth the excess fabric up or down to the nearest horizontal seamline and pin. Then mark the new seamline (g).

Pro's tip:

For seams being taken in the same amount on both pieces, leave the seam stitched as a guide. When the new seamline has been stitched, remove old one.

Changing darts: When you try on a garment, it's simple to change the size and position of darts to achieve better shaping. The general rule: All darts should point to the fullest part of the area they shape, and then end ½″ to 1″ (1.3 to 2.5 cm) from the apex or high point of that area. When making changes in darts, work on the outside of the garment first, then transfer the changes to the inside for stitching.

If a dart starts at a seam, first open the seam at the dart. To widen or narrow a dart on skirts or pants, open and re-pin, making the dart longer or shorter as needed (a).

To change the location or angle of a dart, open and re-pin the dart in the correct position (b).

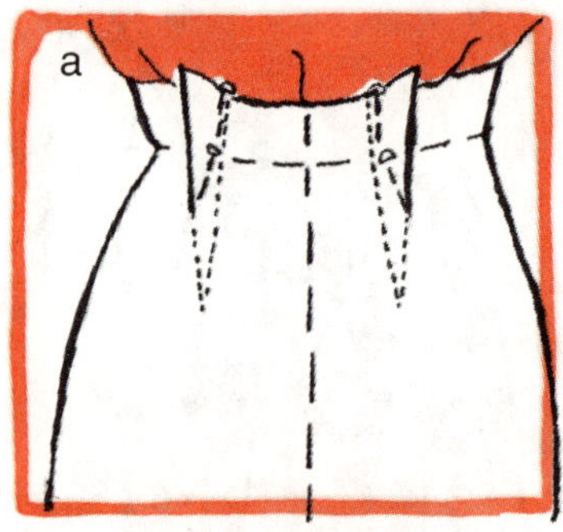

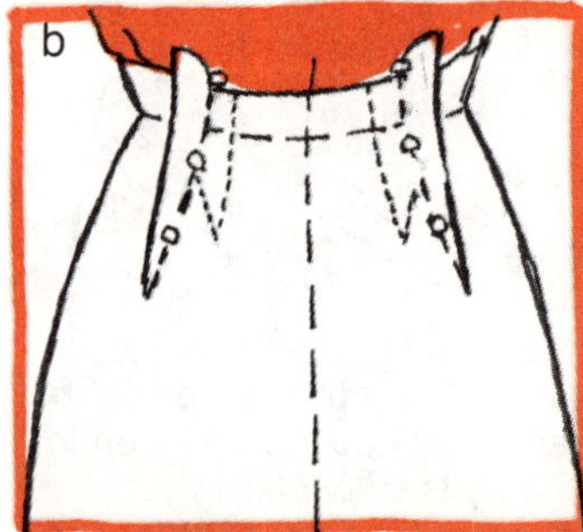

Transferring changes to the inside of the garment: After you have pin-fitted any changes on the outside of the garment (c), you'll need to make them visible on the inside before you can final-stitch. With the pins in place, turn the garment to the wrong side and rub a chalk pencil over the pins to mark the new seamline (d). Remove pins from the right side, straighten the seamline, if necessary, and re-pin on the wrong side (e).

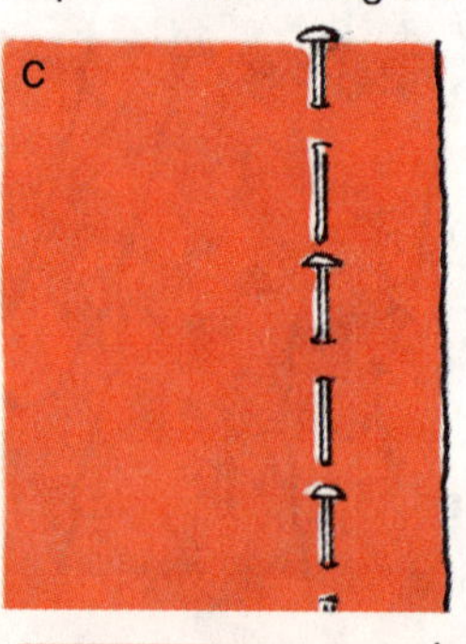

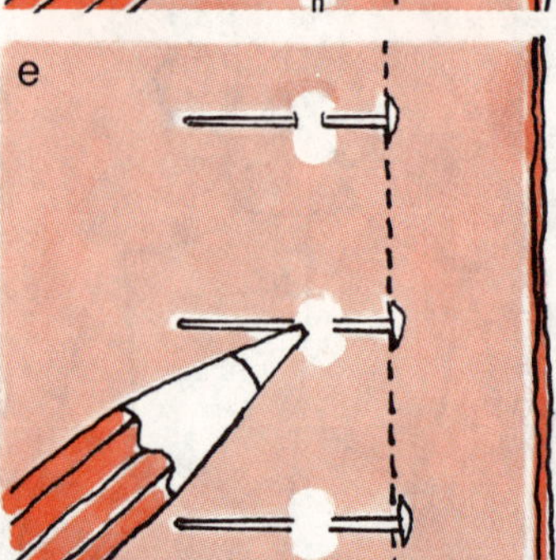

Next, machine baste the new seams and try on the garment to check your changes. Fitting changes on necklines and armholes can be done using the same methods as for seams. Mark the changes with pins on the right side of the garment, then transfer them to the wrong side and stitch.

Pro's tip:

If the seams to be taken in are long, pin a tuck at both ends to mark what to take in, rather than the whole seam (f). This will save you fitting time, and you can mark the entire seam later.

SIMPLE PATTERN ADJUSTMENTS

Width

Follow the order on the chart, page 22. Add paper to pattern edges where necessary.

Shoulder length: For adjustments up to ¼" (6 mm), mark the amount you need to add or subtract on the pattern at the shoulder line. Draw a new cutting line, tapering to the original line above the armhole notch. For adjustments over ¼" (6 mm), see pages 30-33.

Back width: Adjust back *only*. For changes up to 1" (2.5 cm), mark ½ the amount at armhole cutting line above notch. Draw a new cutting line from mark, tapering to shoulder and underarm. For changes over 1" (2.5 cm), see pages 46-49.

Length

Shorten/lengthen lines printed on the pattern tell you where to adjust. You might have to lengthen and shorten a pattern piece in two places—lengthen crotch depth and shorten pants legs, for example. Be sure to make the same changes on all pattern pieces to be joined.

To shorten: Measure up from the shorten/lengthen line the amount you need and draw a line across the pattern. Fold the pattern on the printed line and bring the fold to the drawn line. Pin or tape in place. Redraw any affected cutting lines and darts. To shorten the lower edge, measure and mark the change. Cut away any excess.

To lengthen: Cut pattern apart on the shorten/lengthen line. Place a piece of paper underneath and spread the pattern the amount you need. Then pin or tape to paper. Connect cutting lines and any darts. To lengthen a hem at the lower edge, place paper underneath the pattern. Extend cutting lines and redraw the bottom edge, following the curve.

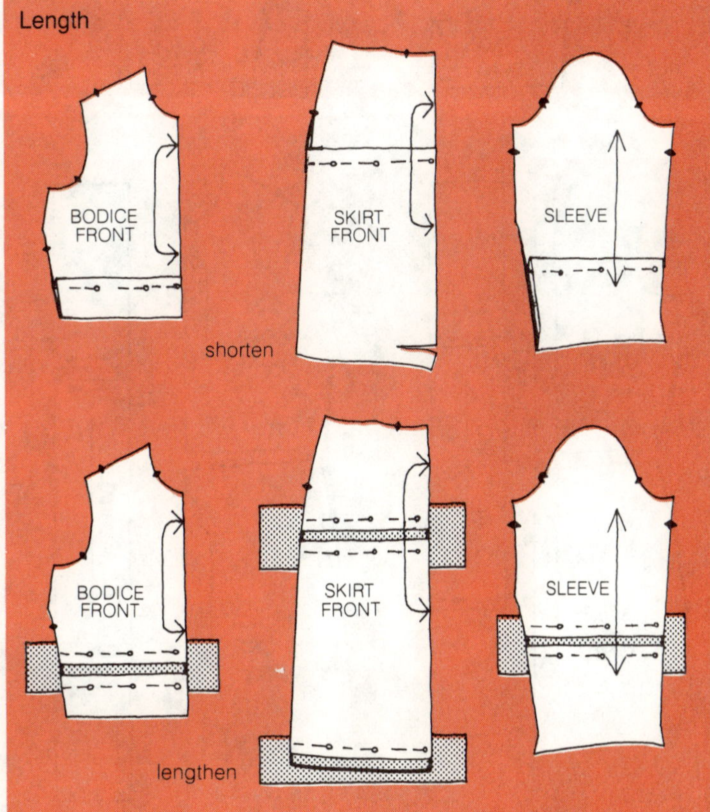

ADJUSTMENTS

To make these basic changes, consult your adjustment chart on page 22 for the amounts to be added or subtracted from your pattern. Then follow the number order on the chart to make the needed pattern adjustments.

Circumference adjustments

There are two ways to handle changes in circumference. One is to add or subtract at the side seams, usually ¼ the total amount needed at each seam allowance, front and back. This works well for adjustments up to 2″ (5 cm).

The other way is the slash-and-spread method, best for making changes over 2″ (5 cm) or for changing pattern pieces with complicated outlines. The easiest ones are shown here;

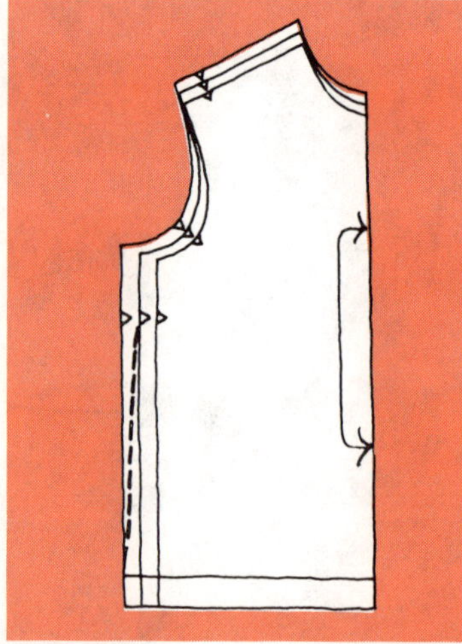

for others see the indexed sections throughout the Handbook.

Simplicity multiple-size patterns, such as Personal-Fit™, or E.S.P.™ make it easy to change circumference. They have cutting lines for two to four sizes, enabling you to make adjustments by simply tapering the line from one size to another.

The circumference adjustments below are shown on the front pattern sections only. Be sure to make the same adjustment on the back sections as well.

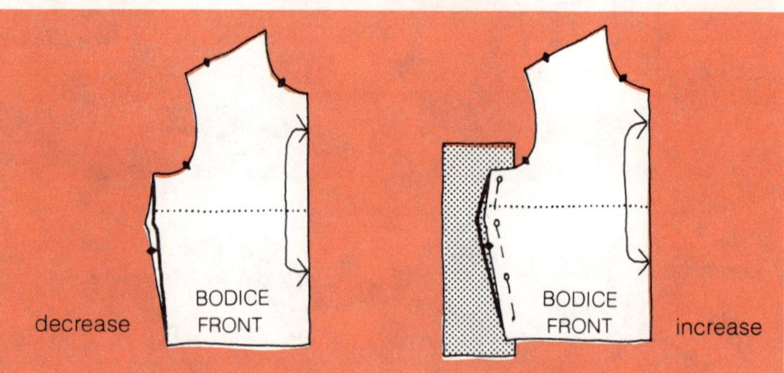

Bustline: To decrease or increase up to 1″ (2.5 cm), place paper under the side edges and mark ¼ the amount needed in or out at the bustline. Draw a new cutting line, passing through the mark and tapering to the original line at armhole and waistline. For bust cup adjustment, see pages 42-45.

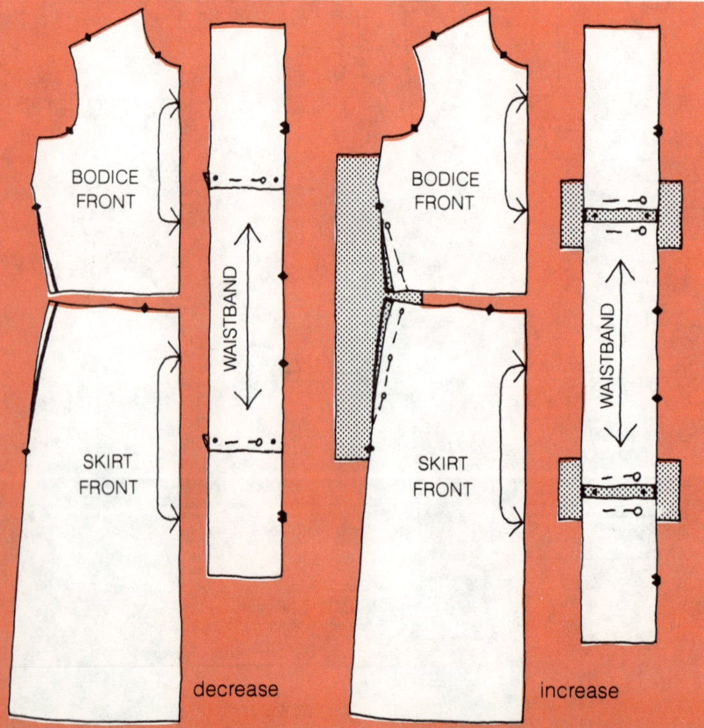

Waistline: For adjustments up to 2″ (5 cm), mark ¼ the amount needed in or out at the side waistline edge. Draw a new cutting line, tapering up to the bust and down to the hip.

To change a waistband, draw lines perpendicular to the grainline at the side markings. To decrease, measure ½ the amount needed from each line and draw a parallel line. Fold pattern on first line, bring to second line; pin or tape in place. To increase the waistband, cut apart on lines, spread apart ½ the amount; pin or tape to the paper. Connect the cutting lines. Relocate markings in center of tuck or spread. For changes over 2″ (5 cm), change dart widths as well, dividing amount equally among darts. Change waistband accordingly.

Hipline: To change hips, mark ¼ the amount in or out at the hipline, using paper underneath for additions. Draw a new cutting line, tapering up to the waist and extending down to the hem, parallel to the seamline.

To increase a hipline more than 2″ (5 cm), draw a line through dart, if there is one, from top to bottom, parallel to the grainline. Cut apart and spread the pattern ¼ the amount needed. Pin or tape to paper. Take in extra width at darts and taper side cutting lines up to the waistline. Redraw the dart.

Sleeve width: Draw a line parallel to grainline from dot at sleeve cap down to wrist. Cut pattern apart on this line. To change width, lap or spread the needed amount. Redraw cutting lines. For increasing sleeve width, pin or tape pattern to paper. On bodice side seam, subtract or add ½ the amount changed, tapering to seamline or bust dart. Move armhole notches up or down the same amount as on sleeve.

Princess styles: When adjusting bust, waist or hip on a princess style, follow the adjustment instructions above, but divide the total amount of the adjustment equally among all seams. As a rule, you'd have six, excluding the back seam. Therefore you would divide the total amount of adjustment by 6 and then divide that number by 2 to get the amount to add or subtract on each seam allowance.

Once you've made these simple adjustments, your pattern should fit you. But if there are more specific fitting problems involved, such as sloping shoulders, for example, the pages that follow will solve these special problems for you.

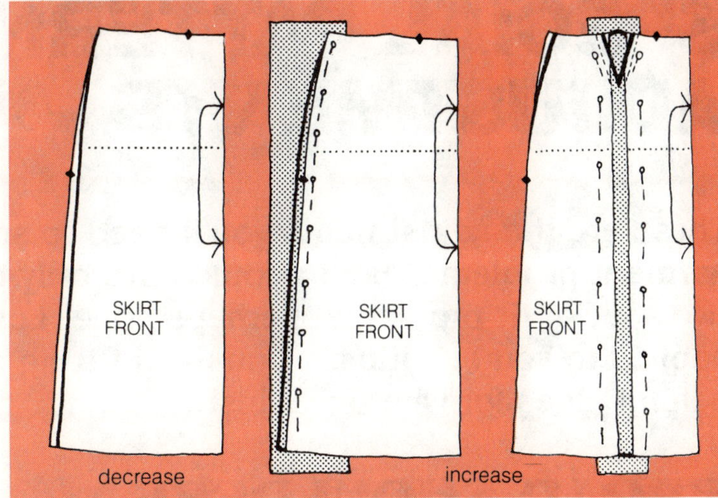

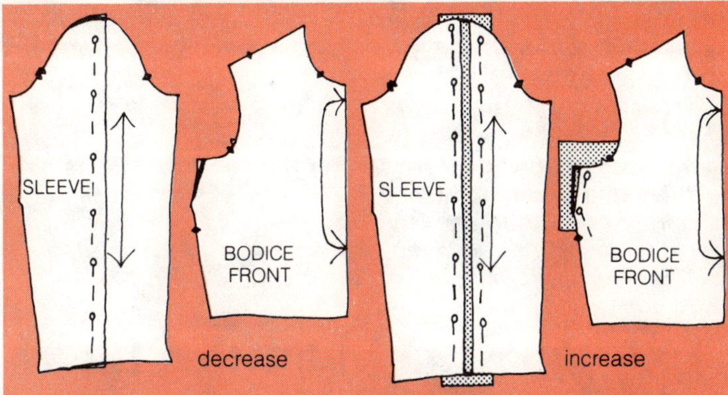

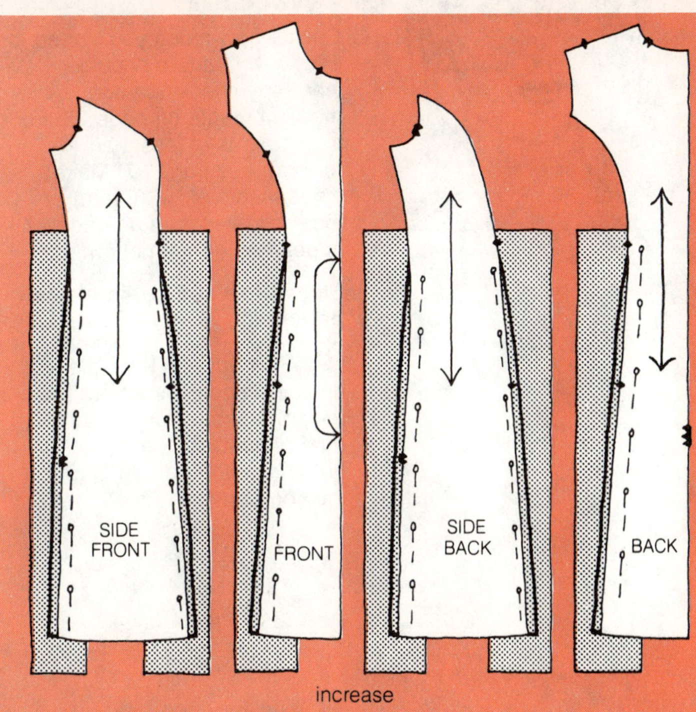

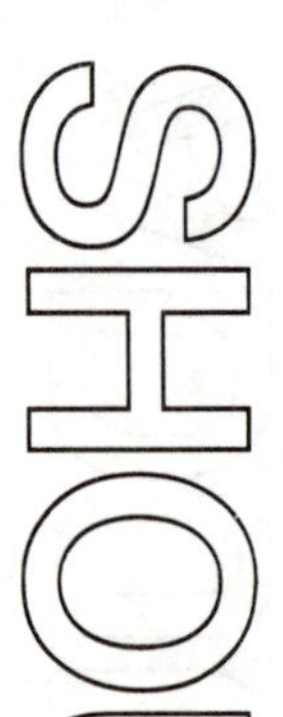

SPECIAL PATTERN ADJUSTMENTS

These are the adjustments you'll need to solve more specific garment problems. Most people have only one or, at the most, two special fit problems, perhaps none. Look for the one that applies to you . . . illustrations and fitting alerts are your helpful clues for what to adjust.

BROAD SHOULDERS

Fitting alert:

If garment shoulder seams are shorter than your shoulders, you'll feel uncomfortable. You will see strain lines across the bodice top, especially when wearing set-in sleeves. Some easy adjustments can be made on the pattern to fit broad shoulders—on front and back for most styles, or on the sleeves for raglan styles.

Fitting standard:

Whether your fashion is fitted or loose, good shoulder fit is a must. The shoulder line should be a straight line on top of your shoulder, extending from neck base to the bone at the top of the arm—unless it is designed to come forward. If your pattern has a dropped shoulder line, the description on the pattern envelope will tell you so.

Adjusting the pattern

Decide how much you'll need to add to the pattern shoulder length by checking your measurements on page 22. For adjustments of less than ¼" (6 mm), see page 27. Make adjustments of ¼" (6 mm) or more as described on page 27, depending on the pattern style.

Sleeveless and set-in sleeve patterns:

1. On front and back pieces, draw a diagonal line from the midpoint of shoulder seam to armhole cutting line above the notch. Cut the pattern apart on the line drawn.

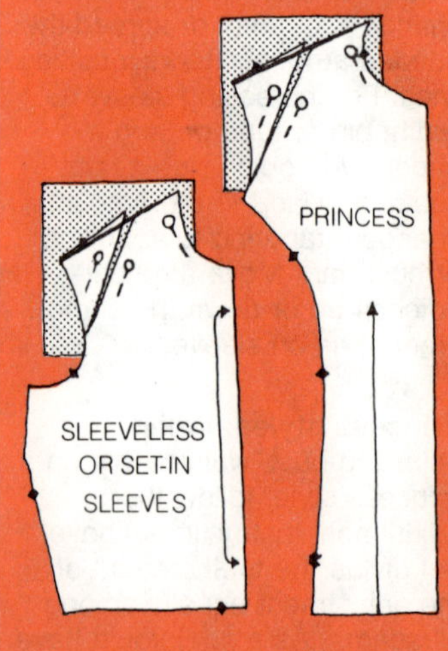

2. Place paper under the cut edges. Spread the edges apart at the shoulder seam the needed amount, tapering to nothing at the armhole seamline. Pin or tape cut edges to paper. Be sure to adjust the facing to correspond.

3. Redraw the shoulder and armhole cutting lines.

Princess styles:
Draw the line so it ends above princess seamline. If the seamline curves high into the shoulder area, pin both front and back sections together to draw the diagonal line. Then unpin them. Cut pattern on this line and continue as described for sleeveless and set-in styles.

Raglan sleeve patterns:
Make the adjustment on the sleeve pattern piece, instead of the front and back pieces.

1. On the sleeve piece, draw a horizontal line between the raglan seamlines, intersecting the dart halfway. Cut the pattern apart on this line.

2. Place paper under the cut edges and spread the dart edges apart the amount you need, tapering to nothing at the raglan seamlines. Pin or tape cut edges to the paper.

3. Redraw the raglan and dart cutting lines.

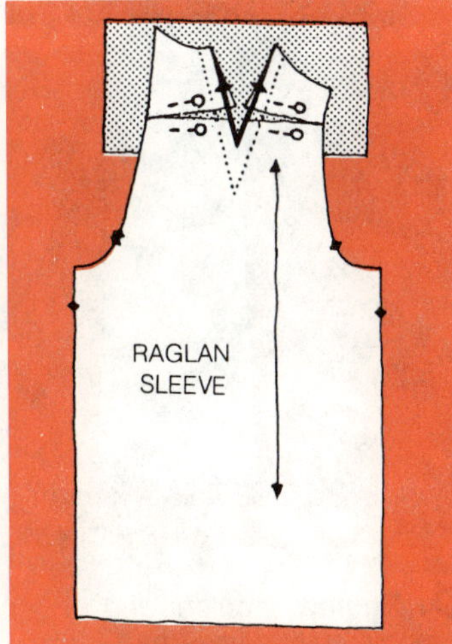

Make a practice garment

Because correct shoulder fit is so important to really good fitting garments, you may want to make a "muslin" or practice garment. This way, before you cut into any expensive fabric, you can test the fit of the pattern adjustments you have made. A muslin can be made of any lightweight, inexpensive fabric.

Fitting the garment

Try on your garment before attaching the armhole facings or set-in sleeves. Pin-mark a new armhole seamline at the end of the shoulder seam; you can add up to ⅜" (1 cm) to the shoulder length. Adjust armhole facing seamlines to correspond. Keep the original seamline of set-in sleeves so you don't remove the ease needed in the sleeve cap. Fit princess styles the same way.

For raglan sleeve styles, you can change the curve of the shoulder dart or seam slightly to accommodate dart or seam stitching and re-pin, letting the seam out up to ⅜" (1 cm).

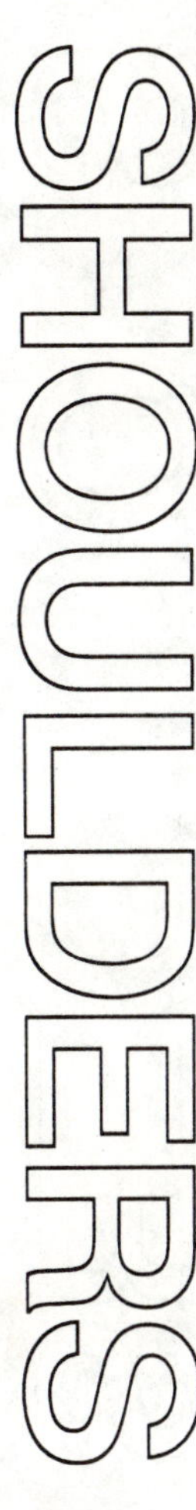

NARROW SHOULDERS

Fitting alert:

Do shoulder seams fall off the ends of your shoulders? Are there wrinkles across the upper part of sleeves? If so, you can adjust the pattern front and back for most styles. On raglan styles, adjust the sleeves.

Adjusting the pattern

Decide how much you need to reduce the shoulder length by checking the measurements you recorded on page 22. For adjustments of less than ¼" (6 mm), see page 27. If the adjustment you need is ¼" (6 mm) or more, see below.

Sleeveless or set-in sleeves:

1. On the front and back pieces, draw a diagonal line from the midpoint of the shoulder edge to the armhole cutting line above the notch. Cut the pattern apart on this line.

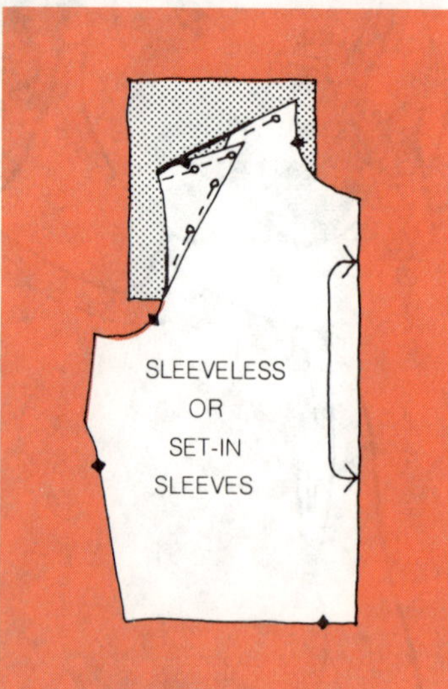

2. Place paper under the pattern. Lap the cut edges at shoulder seam the necessary amount, tapering to nothing at the armhole seamline. Pin or tape the cut edges in place.

3. Redraw shoulder and armhole cutting lines as shown.

4. Trace the same change onto armhole facings and restore their original width.

Princess style patterns:

1. On the front and back pieces, draw a diagonal line from the shoulder midpoint to the armhole cutting line above the princess seamline. (If princess seam curves high into armhole or shoulder area, pin both front and both back sections together above the bust area and draw the line. Then, unpin all the sections.) Cut the pattern on the diagonal line.

2. Place paper under the pattern. Lap the cut edges the amount you need, tapering to nothing at the armhole seamline. Pin or tape the cut edges in place.

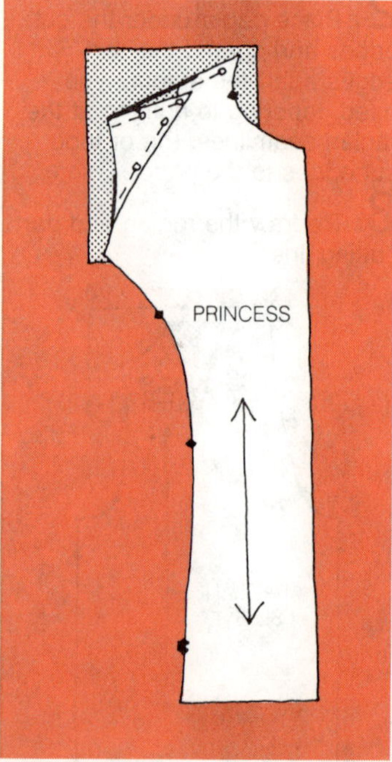

3. Redraw shoulder and armhole cutting lines as indicated.

4. Trace the same change onto armhole facings and restore their original width.

Raglan sleeve patterns:

1. On sleeve piece, draw a horizontal line between the cutting lines of the raglan seams, intersecting the dart halfway. Cut the pattern apart on this line.

2. Place paper under the pattern. At the dart, lap the cut edges the amount you need, tapering to nothing at the raglan seamlines. Pin or tape the cut edges in place.

3. Redraw dart seamlines and cutting lines as indicated.

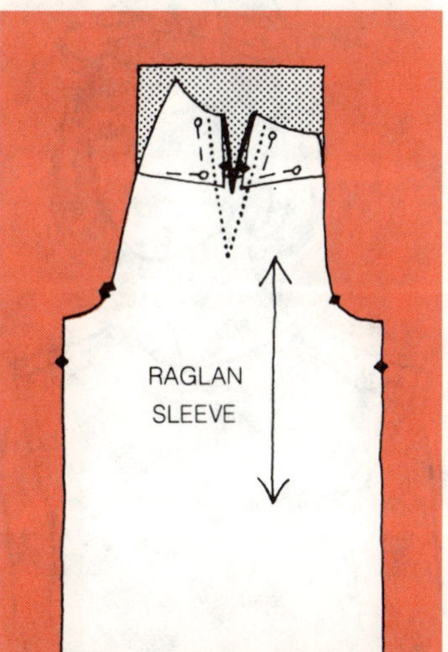

Make a practice garment

Because correct shoulder fit is so important to really good fitting garments, you may want to make a "muslin" or practice garment. This way, before you cut into any expensive fabric, you can test the fit of the pattern adjustments you have made. A muslin can be made of any lightweight, inexpensive fabric.

Fitting the garment:

Try on the garment before attaching the armhole facings or set-in sleeves. If necessary, pin-mark a new seamline at the top of the armhole, taking out the excess width at the shoulder and tapering the new seamline back to the original one at the armhole notch. Adjust the sleeveless armhole facing seamlines to correspond. For set-in sleeves, keep the original seamline to maintain the ease that is needed in the sleeve cap.

On raglan styles, you can shorten the dart slightly.

SLOPING SHOULDERS

Fitting alert:

Sloping shoulders can pull a garment down, forming diagonal wrinkles from the neck to the armhole in both the front and the back of a garment. You will need to adjust the pattern front and back pieces. On raglan styles, only the sleeves will need the adjustment.

Adjusting the pattern

Pin the pattern together at the shoulder and side seams and try it on. Have someone help you to pinch out the excess at the end of the shoulder. One shoulder may differ slightly from the other, but it's best to adjust the same amount on both sides. However, if one shoulder throws off the fit of the entire garment, adjust each side separately.

Sleeveless and set-in sleeve patterns:

1. Mark adjustment at shoulder end, below top of armhole.

2. Add ⅝″ (1.5 cm) above mark and draw a new cutting line, tapering to original.

Fitting standard:

Whether your fashion is fitted or loose, good shoulder fit is a must. The shoulder line should be a straight line on top of your shoulder, extending from neck base to the bone at the top of the arm—unless it is designed to come forward. If your pattern has a dropped shoulder line, the description on the pattern envelope will tell you so.

3. Lower underarm the same amount. Correct cutting line.

4. Correct armhole facings.

Raglan sleeve patterns:

1. Decide how much you will have to lengthen the dart to fit the slope of your shoulders. Mark the new longer dart point.

2. Connect dart lines at neckline edge to new dart point.

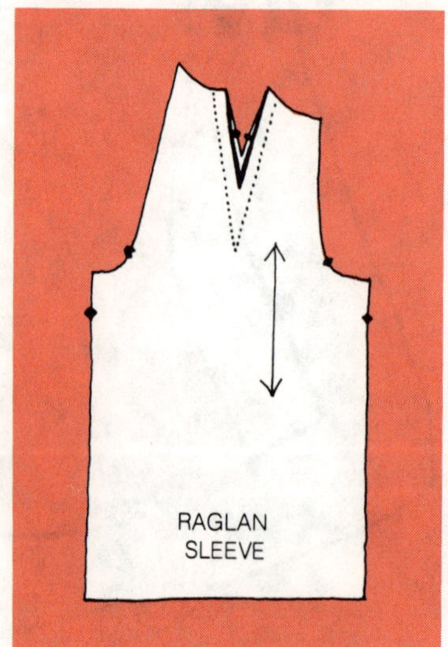

Test the fit of your pattern by making a muslin or practice garment before you cut into your final fabric. This way you can make any fine adjustments you need and achieve perfect fit.

Fitting the garment

Try on the garment before you attach armhole facings or set-in sleeves. Pin out any excess fabric at shoulder seam near the end, tapering to original

shoulder seamline at neckline. Lower the armhole seam the same amount as you removed at the end of the shoulder. Adjust arm and neck facings to correspond, but keep the original seamline of set-in sleeves to maintain the ease.

To fit a darted raglan sleeve, lengthen the dart slightly.

SQUARE SHOULDERS

Fitting alert:

Pulling across the top of the garment from the end of the shoulder area usually indicates square shoulders. You will need to adjust the pattern in front and in back for most styles; on raglan styles, only the sleeves.

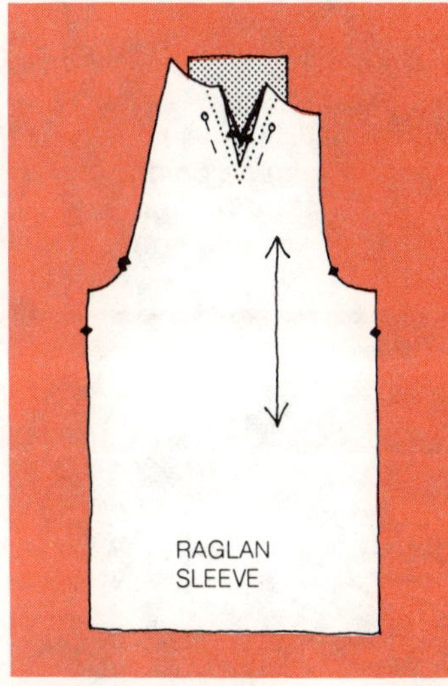

Sleeveless and set-in sleeve patterns:

1. Place paper under front and back; pin. Mark adjustment above top of armhole at the shoulder point.

2. Add ⅝″ (1.5 cm) above mark and draw a new cutting line, tapering to the original line at the neck.

3. Raise underarm the same amount and correct the cutting lines as needed.

4. Trace changes onto facings or sleeves and restore their original width.

Raglan sleeves:

1. Decide how much you need to shorten the dart. Place paper under dart area and pin or tape in place. Mark the new dart point above the old one.

2. Connect new dart point to dart lines at the neckline edge and redraw the dart.

Make a practice garment or muslin. As in other shoulder alterations you may want to make a muslin to be sure that the fit is exactly the way you want it to be, before you cut into the fabric.

Adjusting the pattern

Pin pattern together at the shoulder and side seams. Try the pattern on. Have someone re-pin the shoulder seam for you. Start at the original neck seamline and let the seam out at the shoulder end. If your shoulders are slightly different, adjust both the same amount. If they vary greatly, adjust both sides to avoid throwing off the garment grainlines or style.

Fitting the garment

Try on the garment before attaching armhole facings or set-in sleeves. Open shoulder seams and add up to ⅜″ (1 cm) to shoulder seam at end of shoulder, tapering to the original shoulder seamline at neck edge. Raise armhole the same amount. Adjust any armhole or neck facings to match, but be sure to keep the original seamline of set-in sleeves to maintain sleeve cap ease.

To fit darted raglan sleeves, release the dart and shorten it slightly, as needed.

TIGHT NECKLINE

Fitting alert:

If a fitted neckline is too high, feels tight and uncomfortable, or forms wrinkles at the base of the neck, it's probably too small or may be positioned incorrectly for your body. A minor adjustment on the pattern front and back, plus the facing or collar pieces, will solve this fitting problem.

Fitting standard:

Necklines should lie smooth, without wrinkles, and should fit close to the body without gaping or pulling.

Adjusting the pattern

To see how much you'll need to adjust, pin the shoulder seams together and try on the pattern. Clip neckline seam allowances until the front and the back lie flat at the base of the neck.

1. Mark the new lowered seamline on the front and back, and out at the sides, if necessary. Draw new cutting lines ⅝″ (1.5 cm) away from the new seamline.

2. Trace the adjustment onto the neckline edge of the facing pieces and restore their original width, adding paper to pattern where necessary.

3. If your pattern has a collar, measure the neckline circumference of the adjusted back and front at the seamline and compare it with the original neckline circumference. Then add ½ the total difference to the center back of collar as shown.

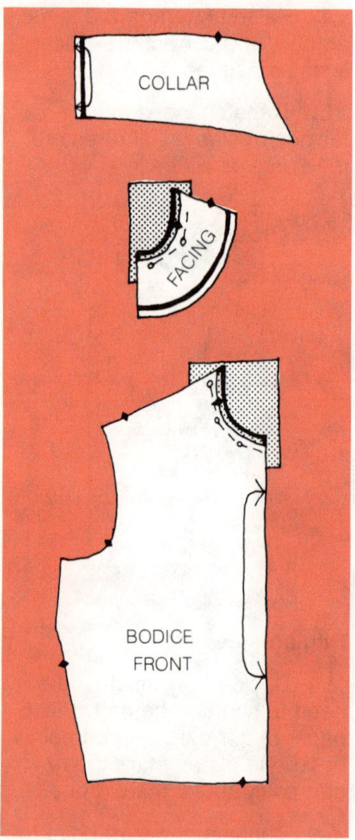

Fitting the garment

Try on the garment after you have sewn the shoulder and side seams and have staystitched the neckline. Do not attach facings, collar or sleeves at this point. Carefully clip the neckline to the staystitching, or past it, if necessary, to make the neckline lie flat in front and back. Mark a new seamline. Adjust the facing to correspond. If you have already finished the collar, it's best not to change it now, so be sure to adjust the pattern first.

LARGE NECKLINE

Fitting alert:

If fitted necklines don't lie smooth at the base of the neck, or if they expose the bones at the base of your neck, then they are too large for you. Adjusting the pattern front and back, plus facings and collar pieces will solve this fitting problem.

3. If the pattern has a collar, measure the total neckline circumference of the front and back and compare it with the original neckline. Then make ½ the necessary decrease at the center back of the collar.

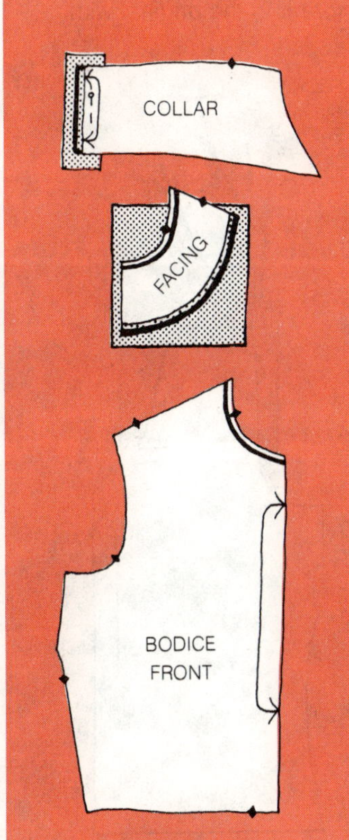

Adjusting the pattern

To see how much to adjust, pin the shoulder seams together and try on the pattern. If necessary, tape some extra tissue under the pattern, then mark the new neckline location around the neck.

1. Mark the new seamline higher on the front and back, in at the sides if needed. Draw new cutting lines ⅝″ (1.5 cm) away.

2. Trace the adjustment onto the neckine edge of the facing pieces and restore their width, adding paper at the edges.

Fitting the garment

Try on the garment before you attach facings, collars or sleeves. Staystitch the neckline, but do not clip the seam

allowances. Mark a new neck seamline up to ⅜″ (1 cm) above the old one. Adjust the facing to correspond. If you have already completed the collar, it's best not to change it at this stage.

GAPING NECKLINE

NECKLINES

Fitting alert:

Do low neckline styles—square, scoop or V-lines—refuse to lie flat, close to the body? When necklines like these gape and feel too large, solve the problem by adjusting the pattern front and front neck facing to get the fit you want.

Fitting standard:

Necklines should lie smooth, without wrinkles, and should fit close to the body without gaping or pulling.

Adjusting the pattern

Pin the pattern shoulder seams and side seams together and try on the pattern. Have a friend pinch out the excess where the neckline gapes. This is the amount you'll have to remove when you adjust.

1. On the pattern front, draw a horizontal line from the neckline edge to the armhole. Cut the pattern apart on the line.

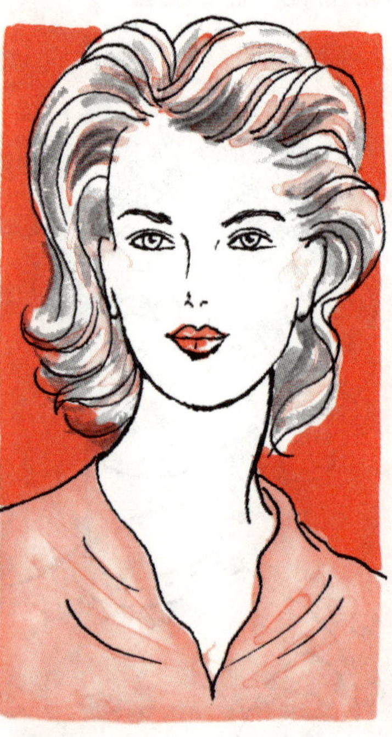

2. At neckline, lap the slash the needed amount, tapering to nothing at the armhole seamline. Pin or tape edges in place. Redraw the neckline cutting line.

3. Trace the same adjustment onto the neckline facing and restore it to the original width.

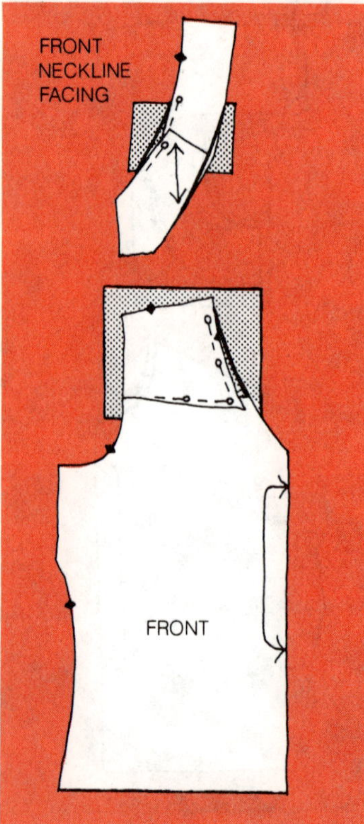

Fitting the garment

Try on the garment before attaching the facings or sleeves. Pin out the excess from the bodice front shoulder to raise it until the neckline no longer gapes. Remove the garment and take up the excess length in the shoulder front seam allowance, making it deeper at the neck edge and tapering to the original seamline at the armhole. The back seam allowance remains the same.

Be sure to adjust the front neck facing to correspond with the bodice front.

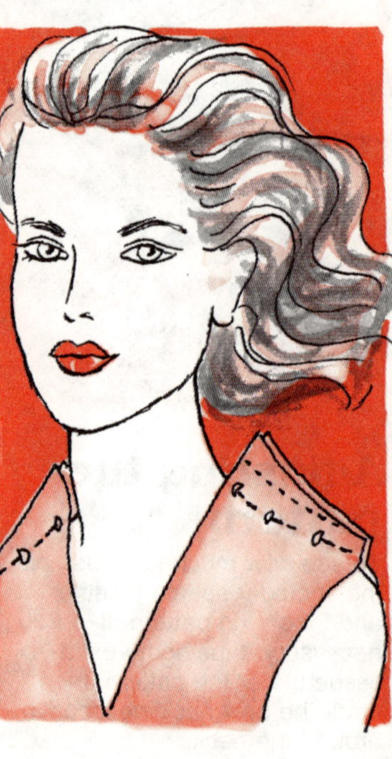

NECKLINE TOO LOW

Fitting alert:

If your low-cut V or scoop neckline is too low and more revealing than you desire, a minor adjustment to the pattern front and back will correct the problem.

1. Decide how much you want to raise the seamline at the neckline. Mark this point at the center front of the paper insert, and remove the pattern. Then add ⅝" (1.5 cm) seam allowance above the mark. Extend the center front line and correct the neckline cutting line of the pattern front as indicated.

2. Trace the same adjustment on the neckline edge of the facing and correct the outer facing edge to restore it to the original width.

Adjusting the pattern

Pin or tape paper to the front pattern piece at the lowest part of the neckline. Pin the shoulder and side seams together and try on the pattern.

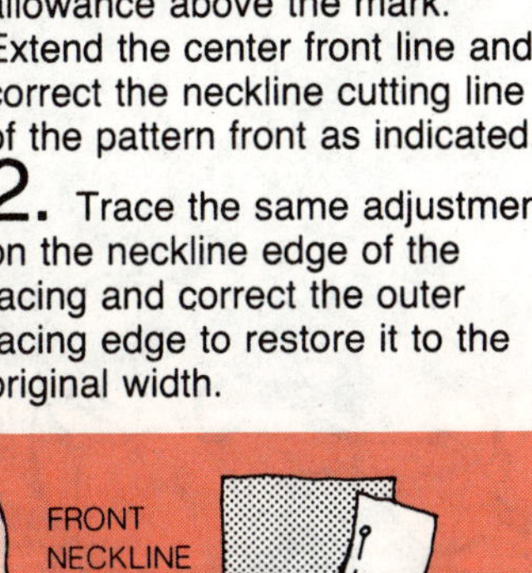

Fitting the garment

Try on the garment before attaching the facings or sleeves. Pin-mark the new center front neckline edge, up to ⅜" (1 cm) above the original neckline. Adjust the facing to correspond with the raised neckline. If you need to raise the neckline further, you can open the shoulder seams and take in only the front seam allowances near the neck edge, tapering to the original seamline at the armhole. The back seam allowances will remain the same.

HOLLOW OR PIGEON CHEST

Fitting alert:

Fitting standard:

Adjusting the pattern

To see how much to adjust, pin the pattern together at shoulder and side seams and try on.

For hollow chest, pinch out the excess length above the bustline where the pattern buckles. This is the amount to be removed.

For pigeon chest, draw a line, slash and pin the pattern to paper as described below. Try on the pattern and spread it to see how much length you will need to add.

Sleeveless and set-in sleeve styles:

1. Draw a diagonal line from a point 4″ (10 cm) below the center front neckline base to the point where the armhole and the shoulder seams meet. Cut the pattern apart on this line.

2. Place paper under the pattern. Lap the pattern for hollow chest, or spread for pigeon chest, the amount needed at center front, tapering to nothing at the shoulder seamline. Pin or tape the pattern edges in place.

3. Redraw the center front line. If necessary, redraw the shoulder cutting line to maintain original neckline measurement.

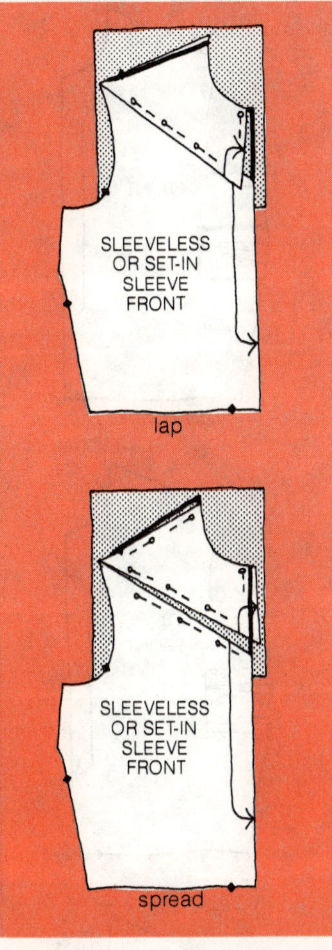

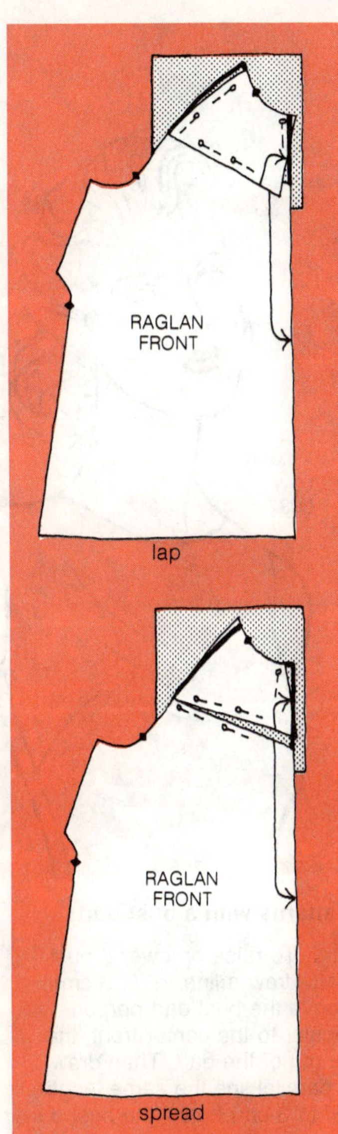

Fitting the garment

Try on the garment before attaching sleeves or facings. For raglan styles, baste the sleeve seams. Beginning at neck edge, take in or let out the front seam allowance only, tapering to the original seamline above the underarm curve. Mark a new neckline seamline, either lower or higher. Be sure to make the corresponding changes on the front neck facing.

Raglan sleeve styles:

1. Draw a diagonal line from a point 4″ (10 cm) below the center front neckline base to the midpoint of raglan seam. Cut the pattern apart on this line.

2. Place paper under the pattern. Lap the pattern for hollow chest, or spread for pigeon chest, the amount needed at the center front, tapering to nothing at the raglan seamline. Then pin or tape the pattern edges in place.

3. Redraw center front line. If necessary, redraw the raglan cutting line to maintain original neckline measurement.

HIGH OR LOW BUST

Fitting alert:

If the bust dart or widest part of a princess curve falls below or above your bust point, adjust the pattern front.

Fitting standard:

The garment should fit smoothly over the bust, without wrinkles or strain. If there are any darts, they should point to the fullest part of the bust.

Adjusting the pattern

Many patterns today do not have bust darts, so fitting may not be a problem. You may only have to make a simple adjustment on these patterns, as explained on page 28. If you need to raise or lower a bust dart on patterns that have darts, check the chart on page 22 for the correct amount of your shoulder to bust adjustment.

Patterns with a bust dart:

1. To raise or lower a bust dart, draw a line ½″ (1.3 cm) above the bust dart perpendicular to the center front, the length of the dart. Then draw a parallel line the same length ½″ (1.3 cm) below the bust dart. Connect these two lines through the dart point.

2. Cut out the box formed by the lines and slide it up or down the amount needed. Place paper under the pattern and pin or tape cut edges in place, keeping the edges even.

3. Connect the cutting lines.

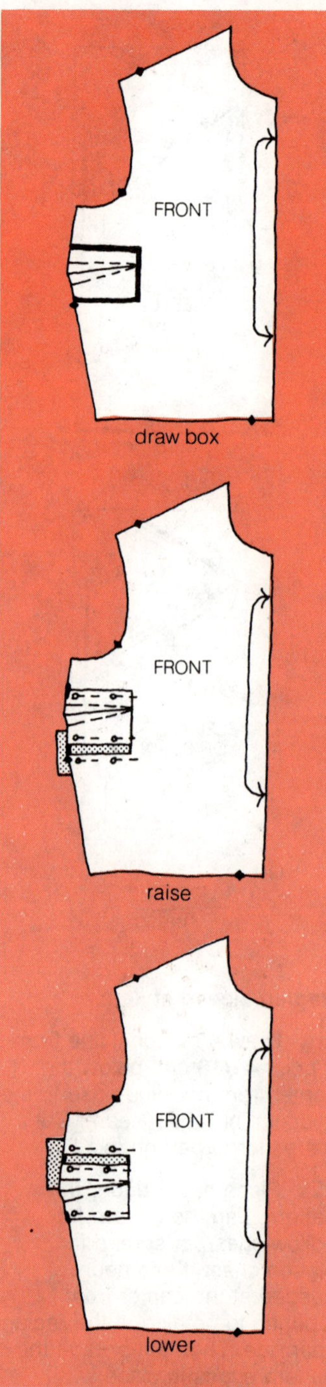

Princess styles:

1. On side front, draw a line across the pattern at widest point of the curve. Cut pattern apart on that line.

2. For high bust, lap pattern the needed amount and pin. To restore original length, cut pattern on lengthen/shorten line; place paper underneath and spread the amount the bust was raised. Pin in place. For low bust, spread pattern apart the needed amount and pin to paper. Make a tuck on the lengthen/shorten line the amount added at the bust.

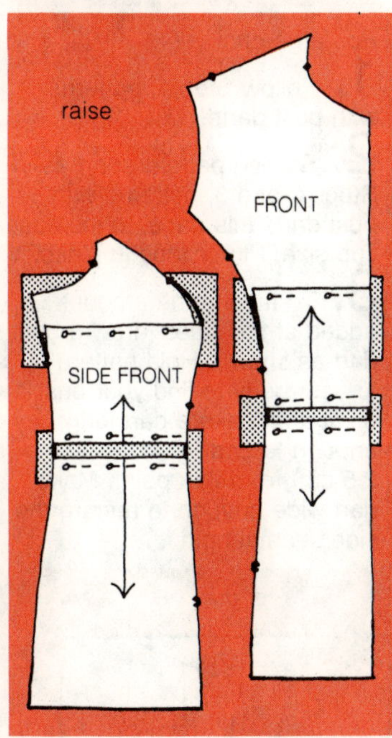

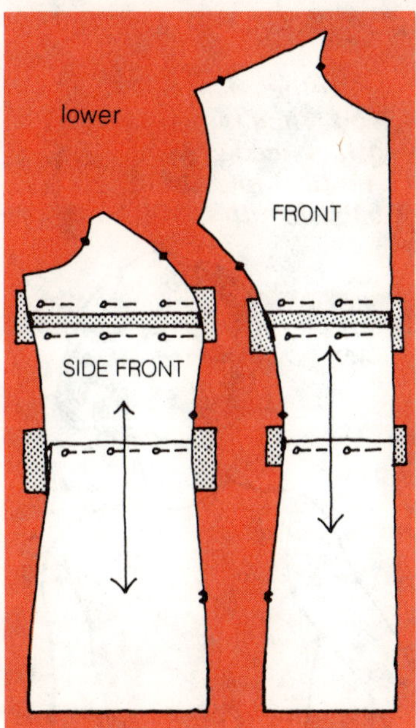

3. Redraw cutting lines.

4. Make the same changes on the pattern front.

Fitting the garment

Try on the garment after you have sewn the shoulder and side seams, but before you attach sleeves and facings. If you are fitting a princess style and the fullest part of the curved seam is too high or too low, open the part of the seam that is affected. Re-pin and reshape the curve by letting out the seam up to ⅜″ (1 cm) at the fullest part of the bust and taking it in above or below.

LARGE OR SMALL CUP

Fitting alert:

If you wear a large cup, C or D, your clothes may pull across the front, perhaps across the back, too. They may ride up at the front waistline where more length is needed. If your cup is small, A or AA, clothes may form vertical folds in front and droop at the waistline if the front waist length is too long.

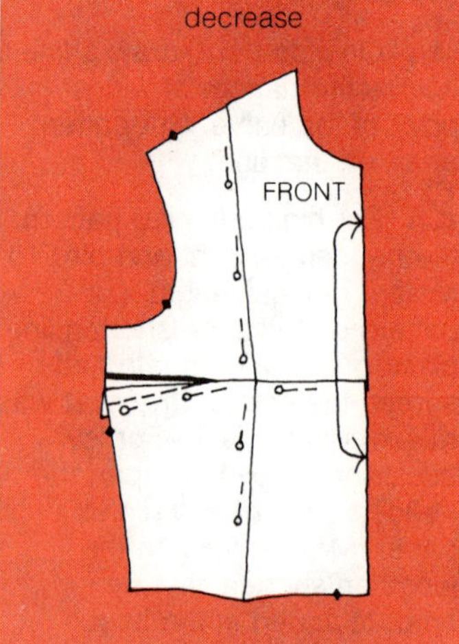

Fitting standard:

The garment should fit smoothly over the bust, without wrinkles or strain. If there are any darts, they should point to the fullest part of the bust.

Adjusting the pattern

To see how much you need to adjust, check the chart on page 22 for your front waist and bust adjustment. Make any necessary adjustments on the pattern front.

Patterns with bust darts:

1. If there is no bustline printed on the pattern, draw one as shown on page 22. Then draw a vertical line from the shoulder midpoint to the waistline (or hemline).

2. If needed, place paper under pattern. Keeping the center front straight, spread or lap the pattern at the bustline the amount needed for front waist adjustment. Pin or tape the pattern in place.

3. Spread or lap the vertical cut edges ½ the amount needed for bust adjustment, tapering to nothing at the shoulder seam and waistline or hemline. Pin or tape cut edges in place.

4. To keep original side seam length, redraw the dart as shown, taking in or letting out the length you add or substract.

For large cup:

1. Follow Step 1, patterns with bust darts.

2. Spread pattern apart as in Steps 2 and 3, patterns with bust darts this page, to increase cup size. Pin or tape in place.

3. To take in the amount added at the sides, draw a bust dart as shown. Hold pattern up to your body to find your bust point and make a dart long enough to end ½″ to 1″ (1.3 to 2.5 cm) from that point. Make dart wide enough to restore the side seam length.

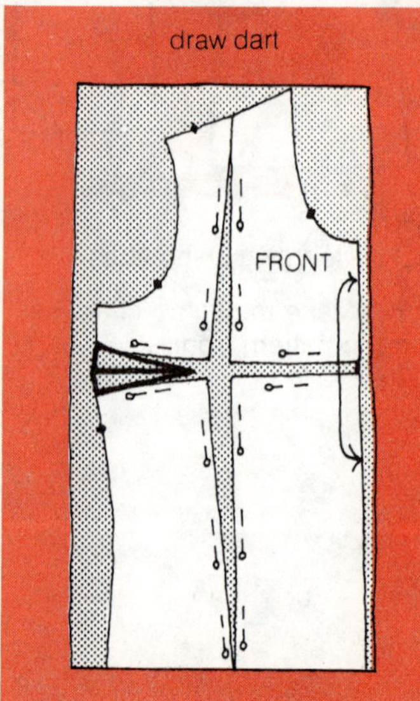

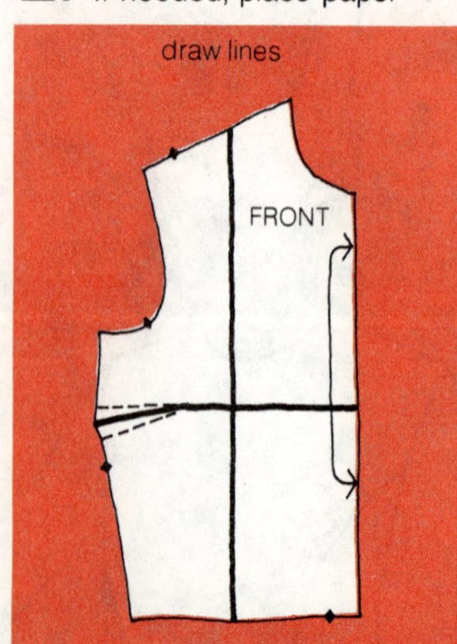

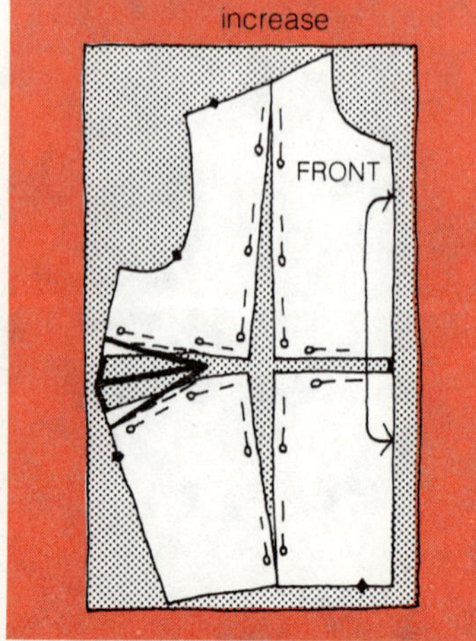

Patterns without bust darts:
See page 28 for simple adjustment for small bust cup.

Princess styles:

1. On the side front, redraw the bust curve as shown, increasing or decreasing ¼ the amount you need on the seam allowance and tapering to the original cutting line at the armhole and waistline.

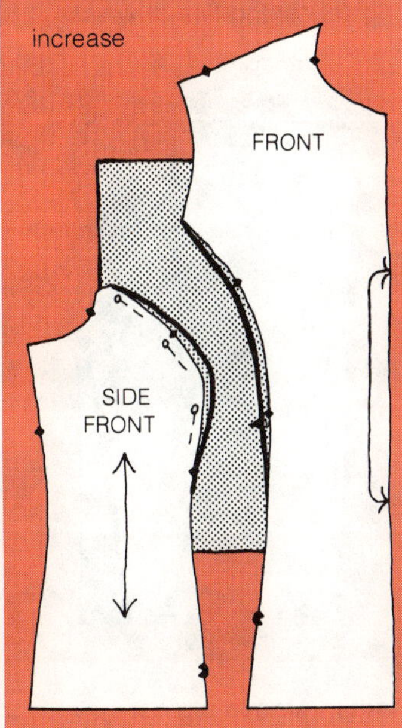

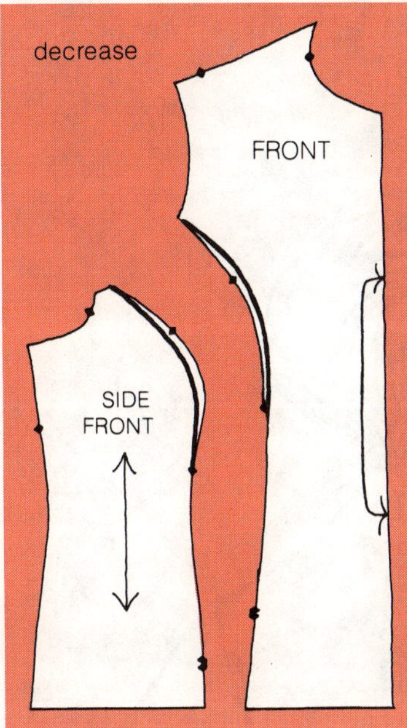

2. On the front, redraw the corresponding curve as shown, increasing or decreasing the same amount as on the side front, tapering to original cutting line at armhole and waist. Note: After adjusting, the notches in the bust area will not match.

Make a practice garment or muslin before you cut out your final garment. This will assure you that your fit is correct when making these important bustline adjustments.

Fitting the garment

Try on the garment after you sew shoulder and side seams, but before you attach sleeves and facings. Open side seams, and front waistline seam if there is one. For large cup, let out front seam allowances only, up to ⅜″ (1 cm); pin a deeper dart.

For small cup, pin out the extra length and width, and pin a narrower dart. If there is no waistline seam, you can add or subtract some of the length at the shoulder seam, on the front seam allowance only.

For a princess style, open the curved seam in the bodice area and re-pin, letting out or taking in the amount you need. You can also let out or take in the side seams at the bustline on the front only. Since these changes take time, it's best to adjust for both large and small cup right on the pattern.

BROAD BACK

Fitting alert:

Pulling across the back means the garment isn't wide enough for you, so you will need to adjust the pattern back.

Fitting standard:

You should be able to move your arms freely as you perform normal activities, like driving, reaching for an object, etc., without feeling at all restricted. Your clothes should lie perfectly smooth, without wrinkles or folds, when you are standing still.

Adjusting the pattern

To see how much width you'll need to add, check the chart on page 22. For adjustments of less than 1″ (2.5 cm), see page 27. Here's how to make adjustments of 1″ (2.5 cm) or more for broad back.

Sleeveless or set-in sleeve styles:

1. Draw a vertical line from the shoulder about 2″ (5 cm) from the armhole to about 1″ (2.5 cm) below the underarm. Draw a horizontal line from the side edge below underarm to meet the first line. Cut pattern along these lines.

2. Place paper under pattern and spread vertical cut edges ½ the amount needed at the armhole notch level, tapering to nothing at shoulder seamline. Pin or tape cut edges to paper.

3. Redraw the side seam cutting line, tapering it to the original cutting line at waist.

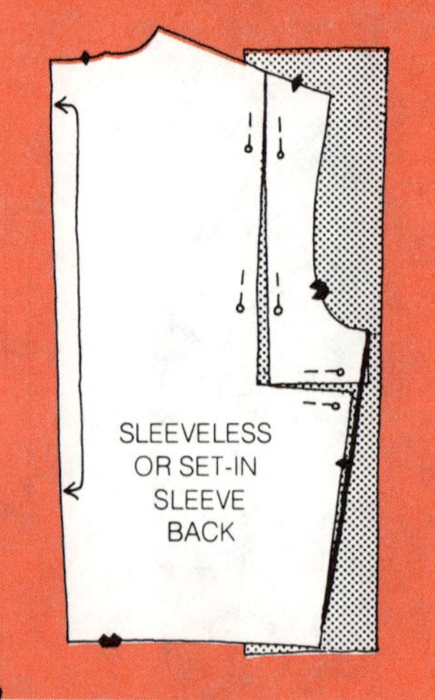

Raglan sleeve styles:
Draw lines as in Step 1, left, beginning the vertical line above midpoint of raglan seam. Follow steps 2 and 3 for set-in sleeve styles, tapering to nothing at raglan seamline.

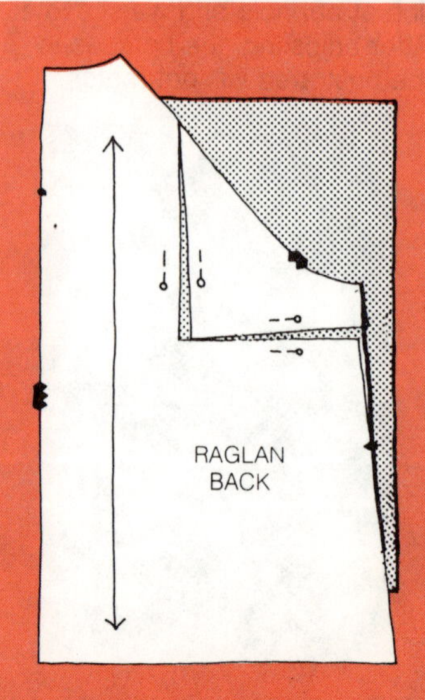

Princess styles:

1. Place paper under back and side back at armhole and side edges of the pattern. Line up armhole edges as shown.

2. At armhole notch, measure out ½ the needed amount. Mark this point.

3. Redraw the armhole cutting lines, tapering from the mark up to the original seamline at the shoulder and down to the side edge, extending out at the side the amount added at the armhole. Redraw the side seam cutting line, tapering it to the original cutting line at the waist.

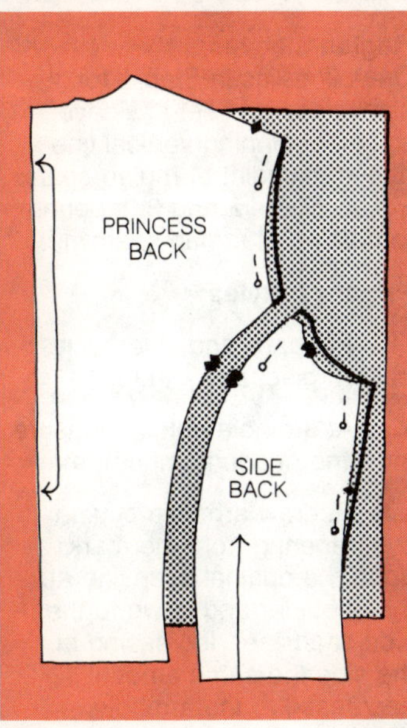

Make a practice garment

Because correct back fit is so important to really well fitting garments, you may want to make a "muslin" or practice garment. This way, you can test the fit of your pattern before you cut into any expensive fabric. A muslin can be made of any lightweight inexpensive fabric. Adding this simple step can assure you that your final garment will fit exactly the way you want it to, and give you a more professional look as well.

Fitting the garment

Try on the garment after you've sewn the shoulder and side seams, but before you attach sleeves, facings and zippers. On a regular or princess style bodice, open the side seams and let out the back seam allowances and armhole up to ⅜" (1 cm). If there is a center back seam, you can get extra width by making the seam allowances narrower. On a raglan style, you can also open up the raglan seams in back and let out up to ⅜" (1 cm).

NARROW BACK

Fitting alert:

Vertical folds that form on the back of the garment are a sign that it is too wide for you. Make the adjustment on the pattern back only.

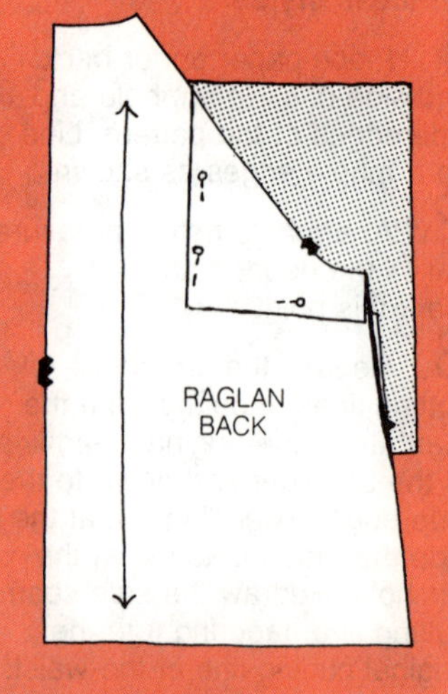

Fitting standard:

You should be able to move your arms freely as you perform normal activities, like driving, reaching for an object, etc., without feeling at all restricted. Your clothes should lie perfectly smooth, without wrinkles or folds, when you are standing still.

Adjusting the pattern

To see how much you need to take out of the pattern back, check the last column of the chart on page 22. For adjustments of less than ½" (1.3 cm), see page 27. For larger adjustments, follow these instructions.

Sleeveless or set-in sleeve styles:

1. Draw a vertical line from the shoulder about 2" (5 cm) from the armhole, down to about 1" (2.5 cm) below the underarm. Draw a horizontal line from the side seam below the underarm to meet the vertical line. Cut pattern on these lines.

2. At the armhole notch level, lap the vertical cut edges ½ the amount needed, tapering to nothing at shoulder seamline. Pin or tape the cut edges.

3. Redraw the side seam cutting line, tapering it to the original cutting line at the waist.

Raglan sleeves:

Draw lines as in Step 1 for sleeveless and set-in sleeve styles, beginning vertical line above midpoint of raglan seam. Follow Steps 2 and 3, tapering to nothing at raglan seamline.

Princess styles:

1. Pin back and side back pattern pieces together.

2. At armhole notch, measure in ½ the needed amount; mark.

3. Redraw armhole cutting line, tapering from the mark up to the original seamline at the shoulder and down to the side seamline, decreasing at the side the same amount decreased at the armhole.

4. Separate the pattern pieces and correct the remaining cutting lines. Redraw the side seam cutting line, tapering it to the original cutting line at waist.

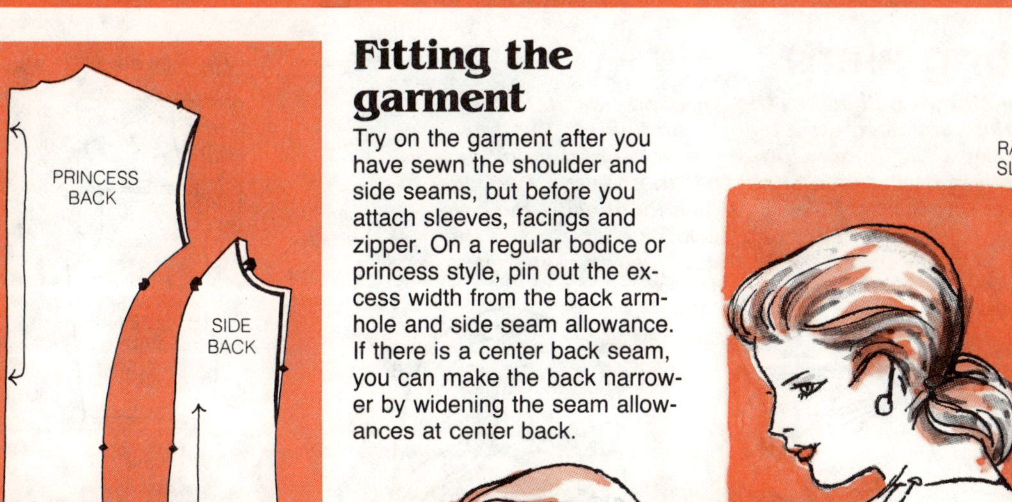

Fitting the garment

Try on the garment after you have sewn the shoulder and side seams, but before you attach sleeves, facings and zipper. On a regular bodice or princess style, pin out the excess width from the back armhole and side seam allowance. If there is a center back seam, you can make the back narrower by widening the seam allowances at center back.

Make a practice garment

Because correct back fit is so important to really well fitting garments, you may want to make a "muslin" or practice garment. This way, you can test the fit of your pattern before you cut into any expensive fabric. A muslin can be made of any lightweight inexpensive fabric. Adding this simple step can assure you that your final garment will fit exactly the way you want it to, and give you a more professional look as well.

BACK

Fitting alert:

If your clothes pull across the back and ride up at the back waistline, you need extra length and fullness to allow for a round back. Or, if your clothes get horizontal wrinkles below the neck in back, that's a sign that there is too much length for an erect back. Either way, you should make the adjustment on the pattern back and neckline facing. To fit the back correctly, some garments may also need an adjustment for shoulders. See pages 34-35 also.

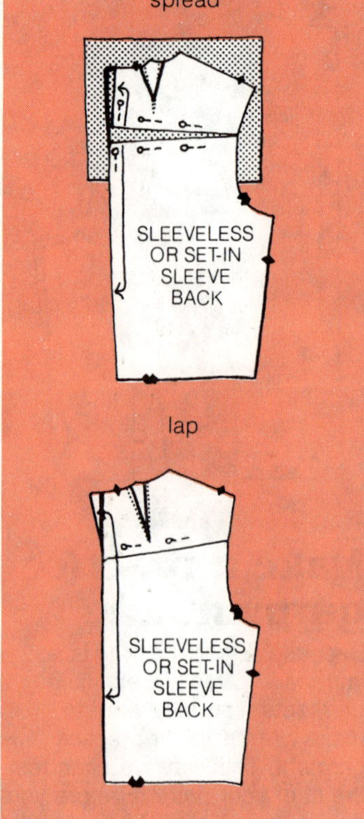

Fitting standard:

You should be able to move your arms freely as you perform normal activities, like driving, reaching for an object, etc., without feeling at all restricted. Your clothes should lie perfectly smooth, without wrinkles or folds, when you are standing still.

Adjusting the pattern

First, see how much length you need to add or remove at the center back. Check the chart on page 22 for back waist adjustment, or try the pattern on.

Sleeveless or set-in sleeve styles:

1. Draw a line below the neckline, from center back to the middle of the armhole. Cut the pattern apart on this line.

2. Spread or lap the amount needed at the center back (use paper under the pattern when adding to it), tapering to nothing at the armhole seamline. Pin or tape in place.

3. Redraw center back cutting lines as needed.

4. For a round back, shorten darts in the area and widen the neckline dart (or add one if there is none) to take up the amount added to the center back neckline. For an erect back, narrow or remove the neckline dart. Change back neckline facing to correspond.

Raglan sleeve styles:

On the pattern back, draw a line below the neckline to the middle of the raglan edge. For round back, draw a line on the sleeve piece from the back edge to the dart. Cut on lines. Spread back evenly the amount you need and connect the lines. Spread the sleeve the same amount, tapering to the dart. This forms a small pleat, so redraw the dart line.

For an erect back, follow Steps 2 and 3 above for lapping. Then add to raglan neck edge the amount removed at the center back. Trace the changes onto the neck facing.

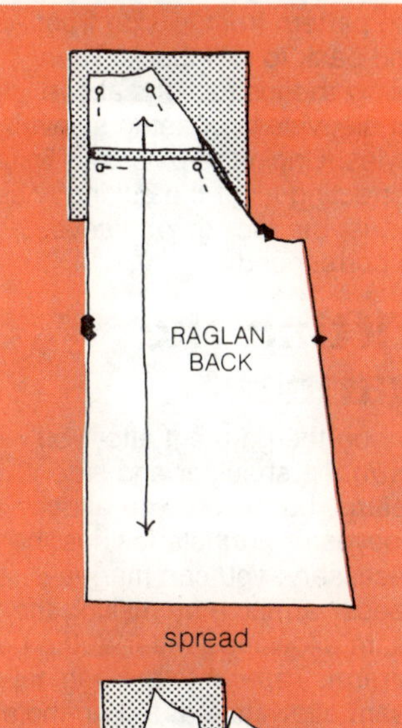

spread

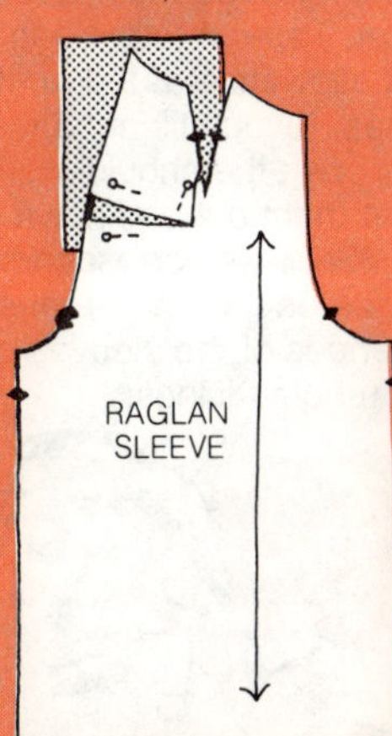

lap

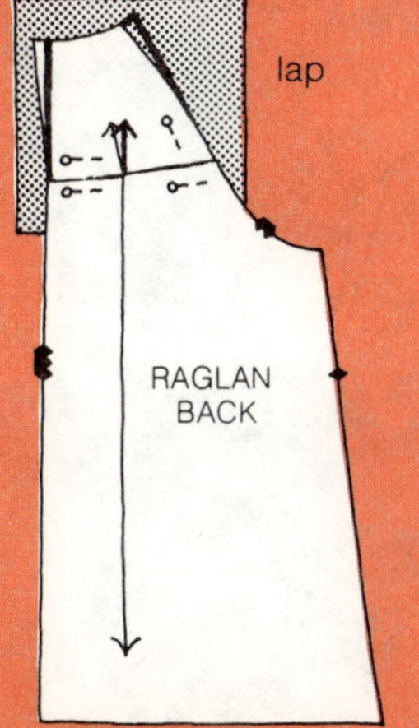

Fitting the garment

Try on the garment after you've sewn the shoulder and side seams, but before you attach set-in sleeves and neckline or armhole facings. Baste raglan sleeves in place.

For a round back, open the shoulder seams. Then let out the back shoulder seam allowance up to ⅜" (1 cm), tapering to the original seamline at the armhole. Let out the back neckline seam allowance up to ⅜" (1 cm).

For an erect back, pin out the excess length from the back shoulder seam allowances, tapering to the original seamline at the armhole. Make the back of the neckline lower by marking a wider seam allowance.

If there is a waistline seam, you can add or subtract length on the bodice seam allowance. You may also have to reshape the neck or shoulder darts slightly for better fit.

On raglan styles, you can either take in or let out the upper part of the back raglan seams.

Be sure to adjust the neck facings to correspond to any changes that you have made.

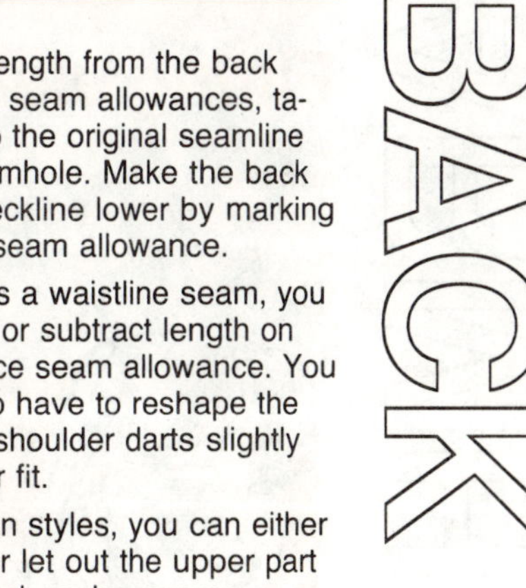

51

ARMHOLES

Fitting alert:

If the armhole is so snug that you have trouble moving your arms, it is either too high or too tight. Sometimes this can be adjusted at the shoulders; see page 35. Otherwise, make armhole adjustments on the pattern front and back, and on facing or sleeve pieces.

Adjusting the pattern

To see how much deeper to make the armhole, pin the pattern shoulder seams together, then pin the side seam up to about 3″ (7.6 cm) from the armhole. At the notches, clip the armhole seam allowance so it lies flat. Slip the pattern on. Mark where the new underarm seamline should be located to give you the armhole depth you need. Then adjust the front and back pattern pieces plus armhole facings or sleeves.

Sleeveless styles:

1. On the pattern front and back draw the new underarm curve, lowering the cutting line the amount you need.

2. Pin or tape the armhole facings to paper. Trace the adjustment onto the armhole facings and restore their original width.

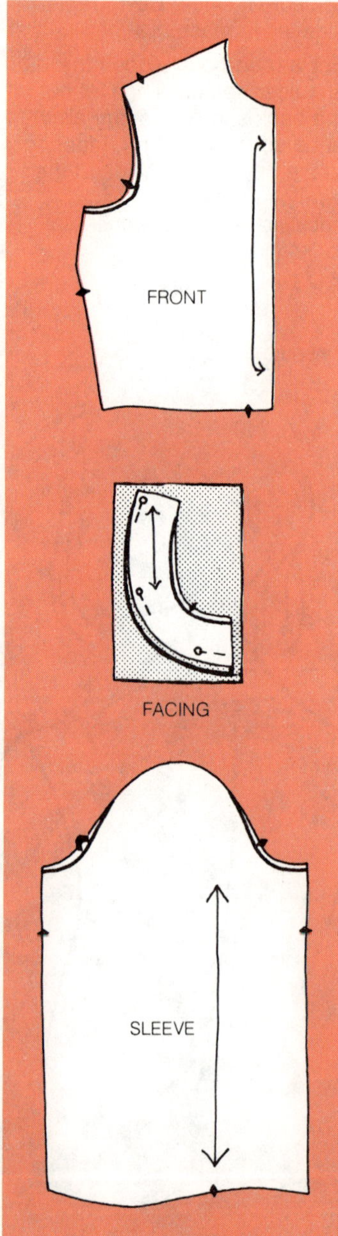

Set-in sleeve styles:

Follow Step 1, above. On the sleeve pattern, lower the underarm curves the same as for front and back armholes.

Princess styles:

Pin pattern front to side front and back to side back. Then follow the instructions above for sleeveless or set-in sleeve styles. Unpin the pieces to finish correcting all of the cutting lines. Adjust the facings or sleeves to correspond.

Fitting the garment

Try on the garment after you've sewn the shoulder and side seams, but before you attach sleeves or armhole facings. If necessary, you can mark a deeper armhole by making the seam allowance wider at the underarm. Taper it to the original seam allowance at the armhole notches. If you still need more room, open the shoulder seams and let them out as shown on page 35. Make corresponding changes on the underarm seam allowances of the sleeves or on the armhole facings.

GAPING ARMHOLES

Fitting alert:

Gaping armholes can be caused by problems in other areas such as the shoulder, bust or garment back. Refer to Sloping Shoulders, page 34, Bust Cup adjustment, pages 44-45, or Round or Erect Back, pages 50-51. If none of these adjustments is necessary, make armhole adjustments on pattern front and back, and on corresponding facings or sleeves.

Adjusting the pattern

To see how much you need to add to the armhole to raise it, try on the pattern as described for high or tight armholes, opposite.

Sleeveless styles:

1. Place paper under the armhole edges of the front and back pattern pieces. Pin or tape to hold in place.

2. Redraw the armhole curves, raising the cutting lines the amount you need and tapering them to the original armhole cutting line.

3. Pin or tape the armhole facings to paper and trace the adjustments made on the armhole of the front and back pieces. Restore the facings to their original width as shown in the illustration on this page.

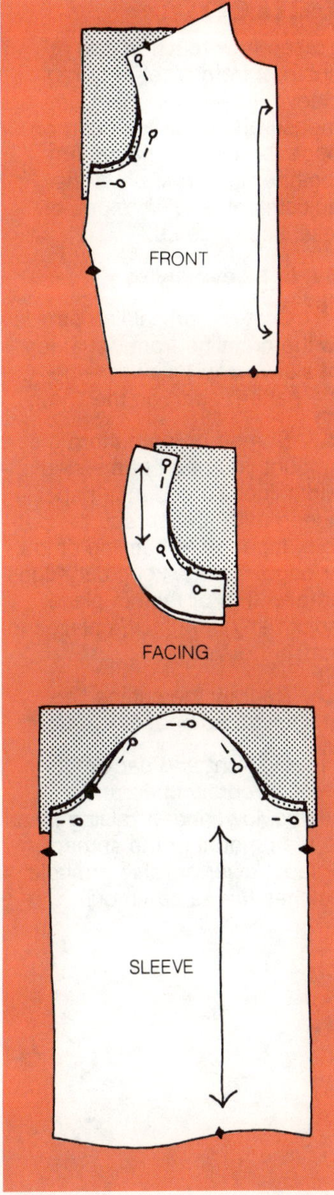

Set-in sleeve styles:

1. Follow Steps 1 and 2 for sleeveless styles.

2. Place paper under the upper edge of the sleeve piece and raise the underarm curves the same amount you raised the front and back armholes.

Princess styles:

Line up the armhole edges of both front sections and both back sections. Then follow the instructions given for either sleeveless or set-in sleeve styles on this page.

Fitting the garment

Try on the garment after you've sewn the shoulder and side seams, but before you attach the sleeves or armhole facings. If necessary, mark a higher armhole by making the seam allowance up to ⅜″ (1 cm) narrower at the underarm, tapering to the original seam allowance at the armhole notches. If you need to raise the armhole still more, open the shoulder seams and pin out the excess as directed on page 34. Make corresponding changes on underarm seam allowances of the sleeves or armhole facings.

SLEEVES

Fitting alert:

If sleeve caps bind, even when you're standing normally with arms down, you need extra room at the upper part of the sleeve. Or, if vertical folds form when your arms are relaxed, then there is too much room and the sleeve width should be decreased. Depending on the style of the garment, make your adjustments on the sleeve and front and back pattern pieces.

Adjusting the pattern

To see how much to add or subtract from a set-in or raglan sleeve, check the upper arm measurement on the chart on page 22. Or, pin the pattern together and try it on. If the adjustment is ½″ (1.3 cm) or less, see page 29.

Set-in sleeve styles:

1. Draw a vertical line parallel to the grainline from dot at top of sleeve cap to lower edge. Cut the pattern apart on the line.

2. Spread or lap pattern the amount you need at the sleeve width line. To add, use paper underneath and spread the pattern, tapering to hemline of lower edge. To lap, keep cut edges parallel. Pin or tape in place. Adjust any hem facing pieces to match the sleeve.

3. Redraw the cutting line at sleeve cap and lower edge.

4. On front and back pattern pieces, redraw underarm curves, lowering or raising them ½ the amount of the spread or lap. Lower or raise armhole notches the same amount.

Fitting standard:

Sleeves should hang smoothly from the shoulder when the arm is relaxed. They should never bind or feel uncomfortable.

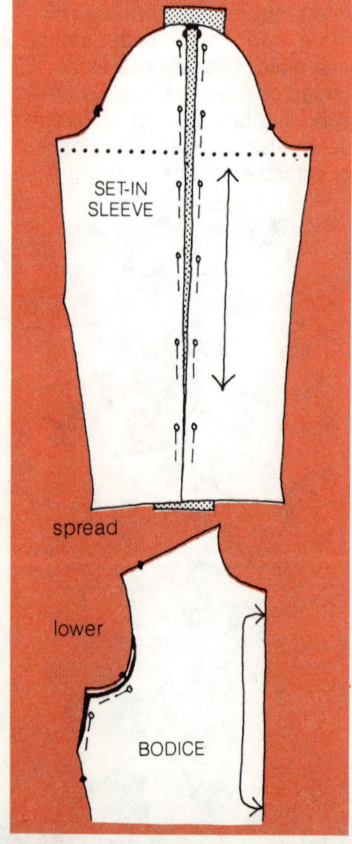

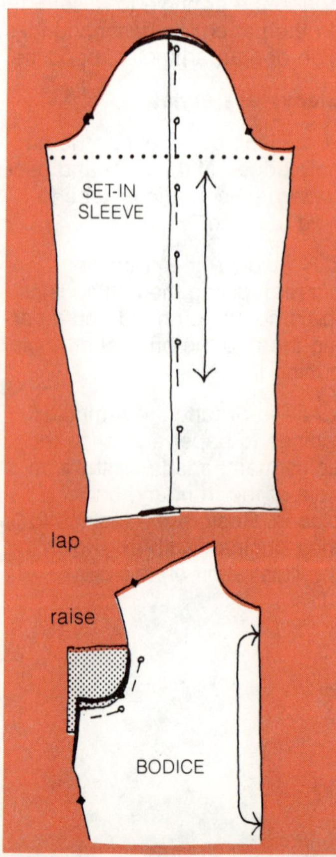

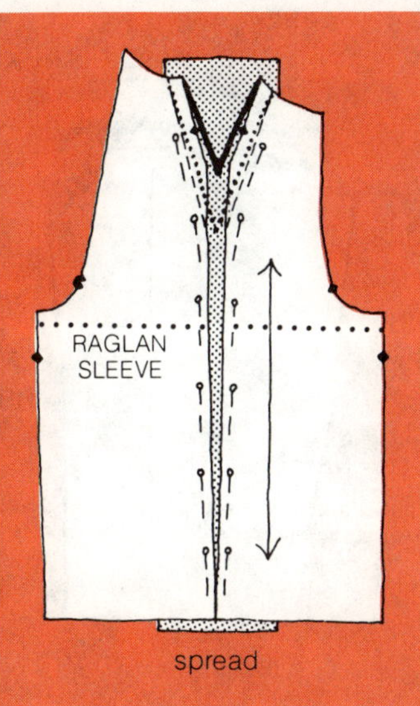

Raglan sleeve styles:

1. On sleeve, draw a vertical line parallel to grainline, from the shoulder dart point to the lower edge. Cut pattern apart on the line.

2. Spread or lap cut edges the amount you need at sleeve width line. For additions, use paper underneath and spread, tapering to nothing at hemline of lower edge. To lap, keep cut edges parallel. Pin or tape the cut edges in place.

3. Redraw the dart wider or narrower, but keep it the same length as the original one.

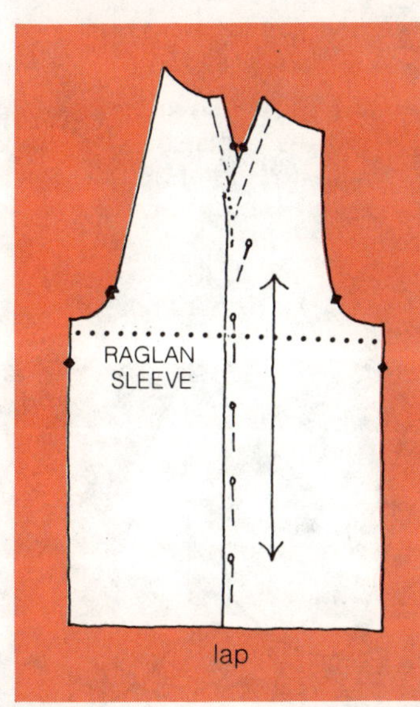

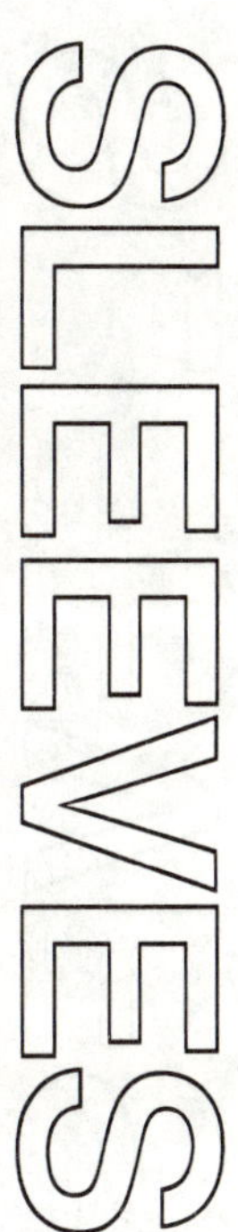

Fitting the garment

Try on the garment after sewing the shoulder and side seams and basting in the set-in or raglan sleeves. Open the upper sleeve seam and the underarm part of the armhole seam. You can let out or take in the sleeve seam up to ⅜″ (1 cm), tapering to the original seamline near the lower edge. Lower or raise the bodice underarm seamline.

SLEEVE CAP EASE

Fitting alert:

In order to have a smooth sleeve cap on a set-in sleeve, excess fullness must be steamed out of the seam allowance. But some fabrics resist steam shrinking, so puckering results. You can adjust the pattern to get rid of the excess ease that causes the puckers. If a set-in sleeve shows diagonal wrinkles at the front or back of the sleeve cap, the ease is not properly distributed. Fix this when you fit your garment.

Fitting standard:

Sleeves should hang smoothly from the shoulder when the arm is relaxed. They should never bind or feel uncomfortable.

Adjusting the pattern

It is necessary to reduce the ease in a sleeve cap when you're using fabrics that cannot be steam-shrunk—those with permanent-press finishes, for example, or pile surfaces like velvets or corduroys. Make the change on the sleeve pattern. First, decide how much ease you'll need to remove; ½″ (1.3 cm) is usually about right. Divide the total amount by 4 to get the depth of the tuck you are going to make. For example: ½″ (1.3 cm) divided by 4 equals ⅛″ (3 mm).

1. Draw a line perpendicular to the grainline across the sleeve cap between the notches and the medium dot at the top.

2. Fold the pattern on the line and make a tuck the depth you need. Pin or tape in place.

3. Correct the cutting line of the sleeve cap as shown.

Fitting the garment

Try on the garment with the sleeves basted in. Remove the sleeve and make the cap seam allowance deeper, about ⅛″ (3 mm), but don't change the depth of the garment seam allowance. If the ease needs redistributing, remove the sleeve between the notches and rearrange the fullness so the wrinkles disappear.

LARGE ABDOMEN

Fitting alert:

Pulling across the front below the waistline means that the garment is too tight over the stomach. The waistline and the hemline may ride up; the side seams may pull toward the front. Adjust the pattern front to solve these problems.

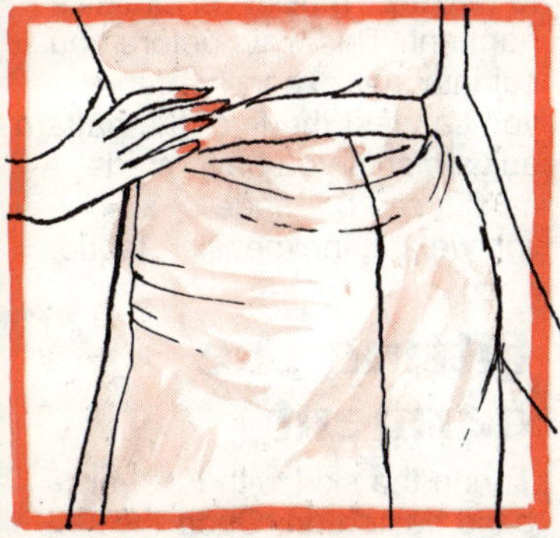

Adjusting the pattern

To see how much to adjust a skirt, slash the pattern front as described below. Pin it to paper and try on, spreading it as needed. For a one-piece dress, pin pattern together and try it on; then estimate how much to add on between waist and hip.

Skirt:

1. On the pattern front, draw a line parallel to the grainline, through the center of the dart from waist to hem. Draw another line midway between the waist-line and hipline from center front to side edge. Cut the pattern apart on the lines.

2. Place paper under the pattern. Spread horizontal cut edges the amount needed at the center front, tapering to side seam. Spread vertical edges ½ the amount needed, keeping them parallel. Pin or tape.

3. Connect cutting lines or foldlines. Redraw dart.

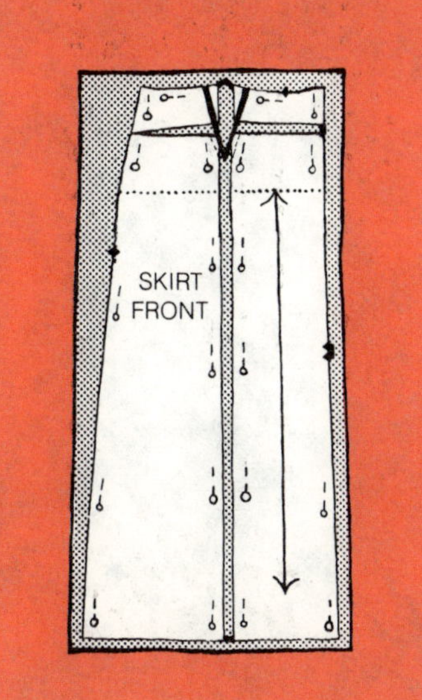

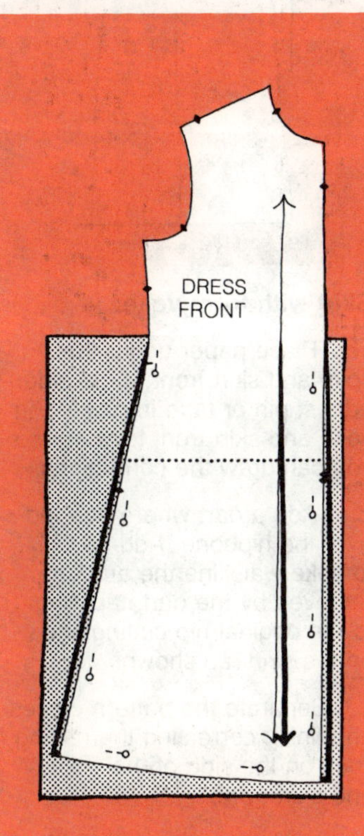

One-piece dress:
Place paper under the pattern. At center front seam and sides, measure out ¼ the needed amount between waistline and hip. Redraw the cutting lines and correct the grainline. If there's no center front seam, add on ½ the needed amount to the sides.

Fitting the garment

Try on a skirt after you've sewn the darts and vertical seams, and have basted the waistband on. Remove the waistband in front and open the side seams above the hipline. Let out the center front seam, if any, and the front seam allowances of the side seams, up to ⅜″ (1 cm) each. For added length, let out the skirt waistline seam allow-ance up to ⅜″ (1 cm), or lower the hemline at the center front. Shorten darts, if needed. On a one-piece dress, let out the side seams and center front seam; lower center front hemline.

Fitting standard:

Clothes should be roomy enough so there is no sign of strain across the abdomen, trim enough so there are no folds or bagging.

PROTRUDING HIPBONES

Fitting alert:

On close-fitting garments, especially those that are made of soft, clingy fabrics, the darts may not point to the hipbone. By adjusting the position of the darts on the pattern front, or sometimes on the garment, you can get better fit.

Adjusting the pattern

To see where to adjust, try on the pattern and check the hipbone locations. This is important, as left and right sides may not be identical.

Skirt:

1. On pattern front, move the dart toward the hipbone and widen it to add the needed fullness over the hipbones.

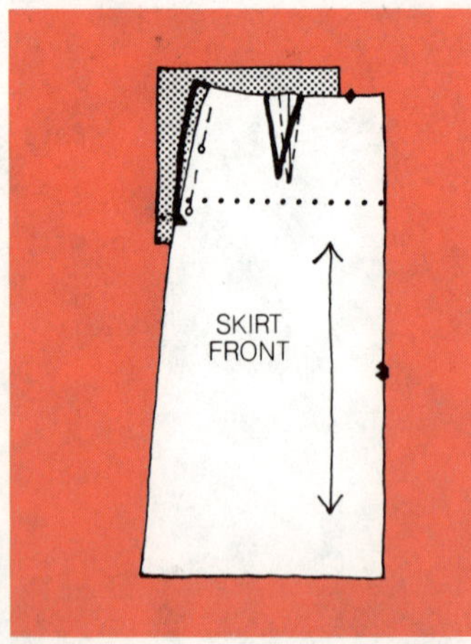

2. Place paper under the pattern. To maintain the waist measurement, add on at the side waistline the same amount you added to the dart. Taper the line to the hip.

Skirt with front yoke:

1. Place paper under the yoke and skirt front at the side edges; pin or tape in place. Pin yoke and skirt front together so you can draw the corrections.

2. Add a dart where needed over the hipbone. Add on to yoke waistline the amount removed by the dart, tapering to the original hip cutting line on the skirt, as shown.

3. Separate the pattern pieces and finish correcting the cutting lines on the side of the yoke and skirt front.

Make a practice garment

Because correct hipline fit is so important to really good fitting garments, you may want to make a "muslin" or practice garment. This way, before you cut into any expensive fabric, you can test the fit of the pattern adjustments you have made. A muslin can be made of any lightweight, inexpensive fabric.

Fitting the garment

Try on the skirt with the waistband basted on. Open the waistband seam, front darts and side seams above the hips. Re-pin wider darts, pointing to the hipbones. For a yoke, add a dart over each hipbone. Let out front side seam allowances at the waist up to ⅜" (1 cm).

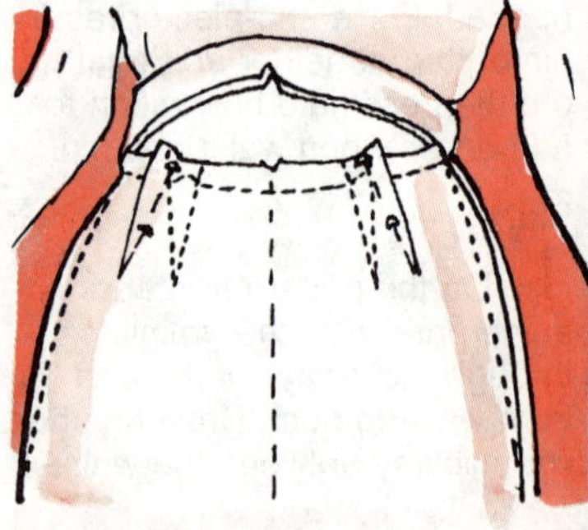

ONE HIGH HIP

Fitting alert:

If a hemline is higher on one side and the center front isn't vertical, it's probably because one hip is much higher than the other. If there's only a slight difference, make the adjustment when you fit. Otherwise, you should adjust the pattern.

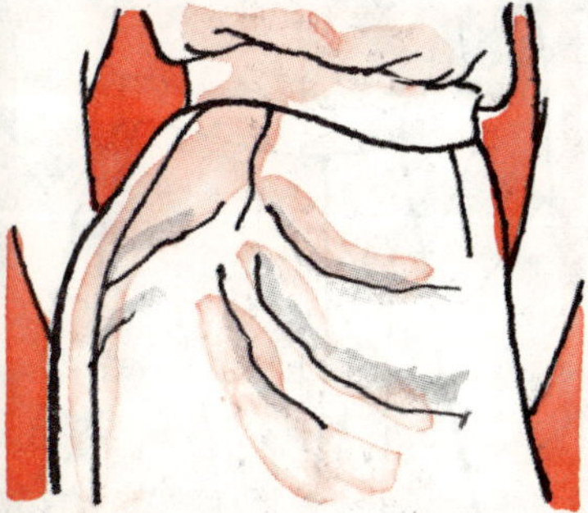

Adjusting the pattern

To see how much to adjust, tie a string around your waist, then measure over each hip from string to the floor. The difference is the amount you need to adjust the pattern front and back.

Skirt or two-piece dress:

1. Make duplicates of the front and back pattern pieces and transfer all markings. Adjust only the piece for the high hip side.

2. On the pattern front and back draw a horizontal line above the hipline. Cut pattern apart on the line.

3. Place paper under the pattern and spread hip edge the amount you need, tapering to nothing at the center front. Pin the pattern to the paper.

4. Straighten the center front cutting line. Then connect the side cutting line, adding to the side waist the amount taken away at the center front.

5. Adjust back the same way. Cut out garment sections separately. To cut pattern on fold, open fabric, right side up. Place pattern center edges together and cut as one section.

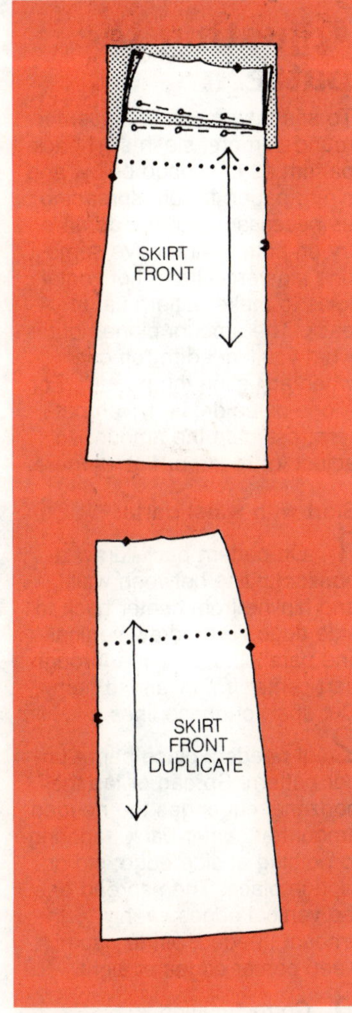

One-piece dress:
Follow Step 1, skirt. Place paper under pattern. On front and back pieces, redraw the cutting line for high hip as shown. Then follow Step 5, skirt.

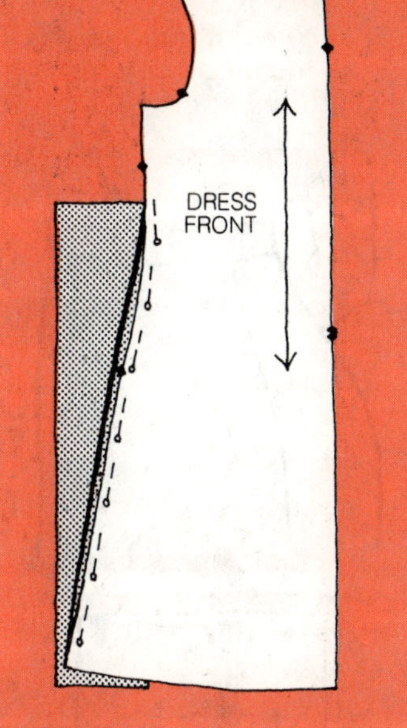

Fitting the garment

Try on the garment with side and waistline seams, or waistband, basted. Open the waistline seam, or remove waistband, in front and back on the high hip side. Let out the skirt waistline seam allowance up to ⅜" (1 cm). If needed, mark a narrower hem allowance on that side. Trim evenly before hemming. On a one-piece dress, open the side seam on the high hip side; let out the seam at high hip up to ⅜" (1 cm), tapering to original seam above and below. Adjust hem if necessary.

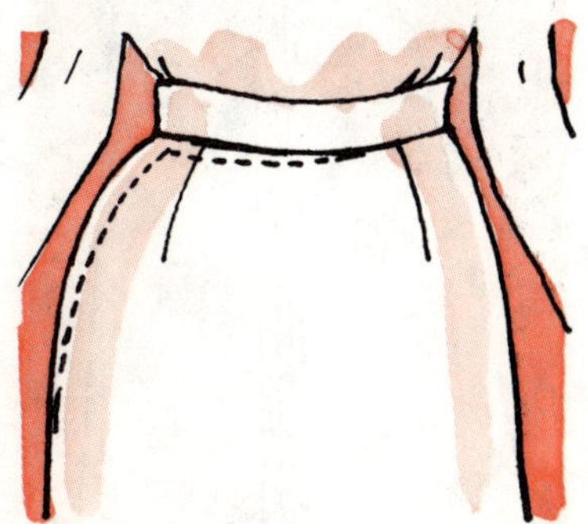

ROUND OR FLAT DERRIÈRE

Fitting alert:

If clothes are too tight over the derrière, side seams may pull toward the back, and the back waist and hemline may ride up. If you're very flat in back, your clothes can sag or bag because there's too much fullness. Either way, you can easily adjust the pattern back to fit.

Fitting standard:

Clothes should fit smoothly over the seat—no bagging, pulling or wrinkling—and should allow you to sit comfortably.

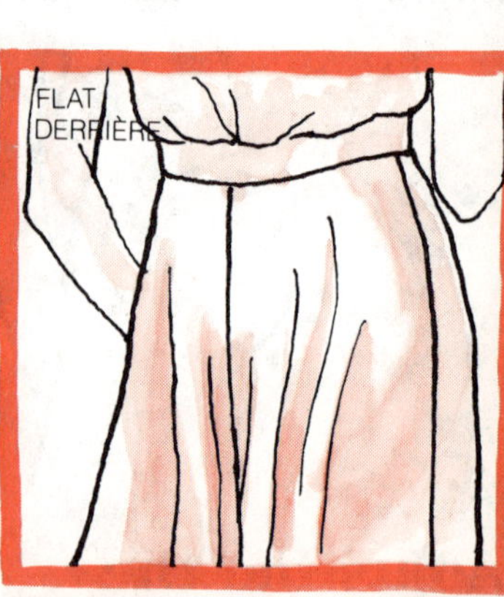

Adjusting the pattern

To see how much to adjust for round derrière, slash skirt back pattern as described below and pin to paper; try on, spreading as necessary. For flat derrière, try on pattern and have someone pin vertical and horizontal folds to make pattern flat in back. The amount pinned out is what you'll need to remove when adjusting the pattern. For a one-piece dress, try on pattern; estimate the amount to adjust for round or flat derrière.

Skirt with waist darts:

1. On pattern back, draw a horizontal line between waist and hipline from center back to side edge. Then draw vertical line parallel to grainline through dart center from waist to hem. Cut apart on these lines.

2. If needed, place paper under pattern. Spread or lap the horizonal cut edges the needed amount at center back, tapering to nothing at side edge; pin or tape in place. Then spread or lap vertical edges evenly ½ the amount needed; pin to paper. Keep center edges straight.

3. Correct cutting lines. Redraw dart, making it narrower or wider to maintain waist size, and shorter or longer, as needed.

Skirt with yoke:

1. Pin yoke and skirt back pieces together. Draw vertical line parallel to grainline through middle of pattern from waist to hem. Unpin and cut pattern pieces apart on line.

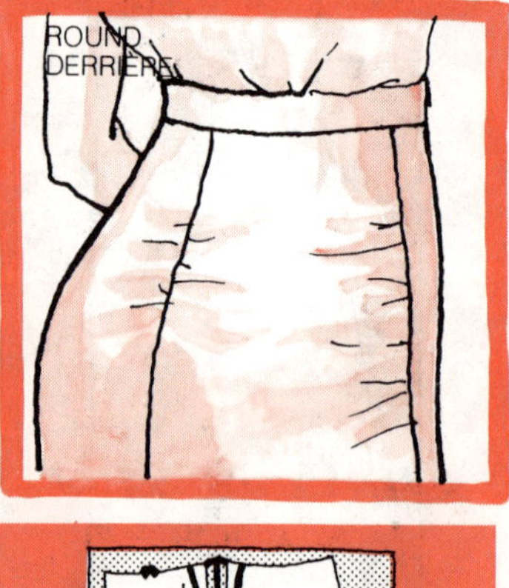

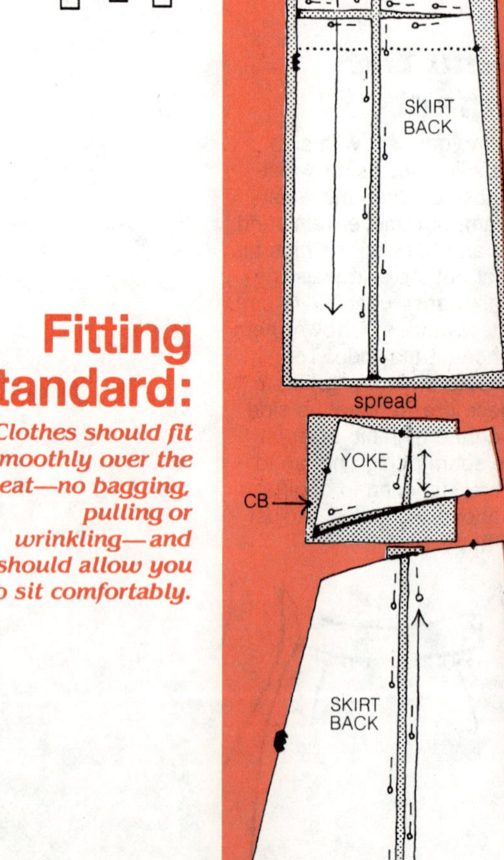

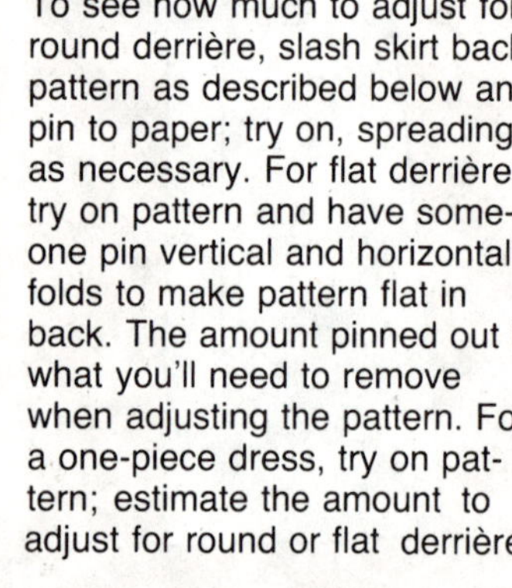

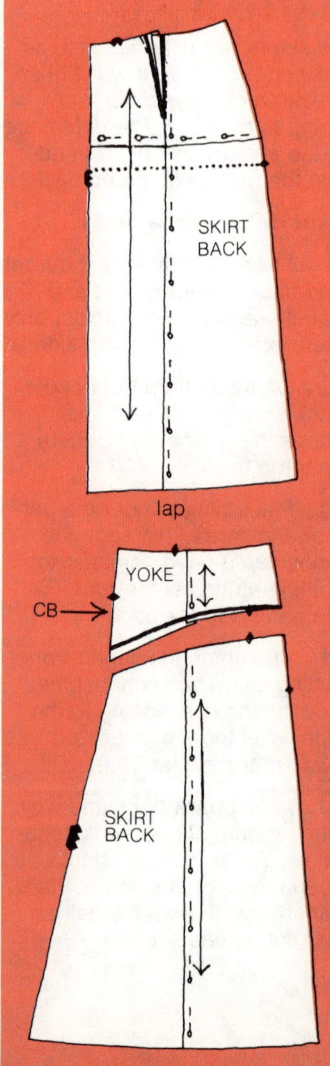

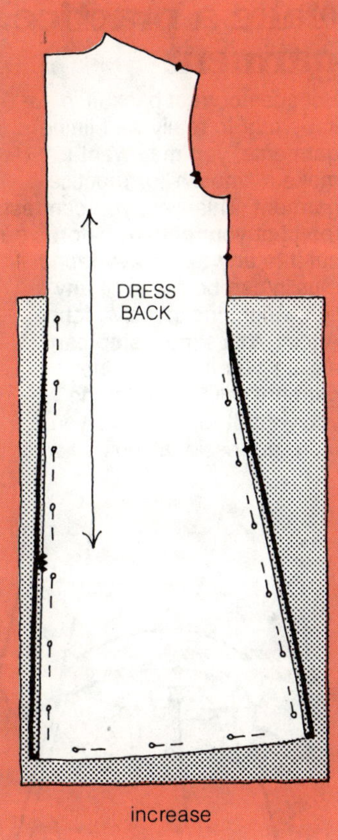

2. If needed, place paper under pattern. Spread or lap yoke ½ the needed amount at lower edge, tapering to nothing at seamline. Spread or lap skirt same amount, keeping edges parallel; pin in place and correct cutting lines. Add or take off at lower edge of yoke, starting at center back, and tapering to nothing at side.

One-piece dress:

If needed, place paper under pattern. Redraw center back and side cutting lines, increasing or decreasing ¼ the needed amount, tapering to original cutting line above and straight down to hemline. If there's no center back seam, add or take off ½ the amount at sides.

Fitting the garment

Try on garments after sewing darts and major seams. For a skirt, baste waistband on. Open center back and side seams from waist to just below hipline; open waistband seam in back. Let out or take in center back and back seams at sides, tapering to original seam at waist. Raise or lower back waistline, if there is one, by making the seam allowance narrower or deeper. You may have to shorten or lengthen the darts to fit the curve better. If garment back is still too short or long, adjust the hemline slightly as needed.

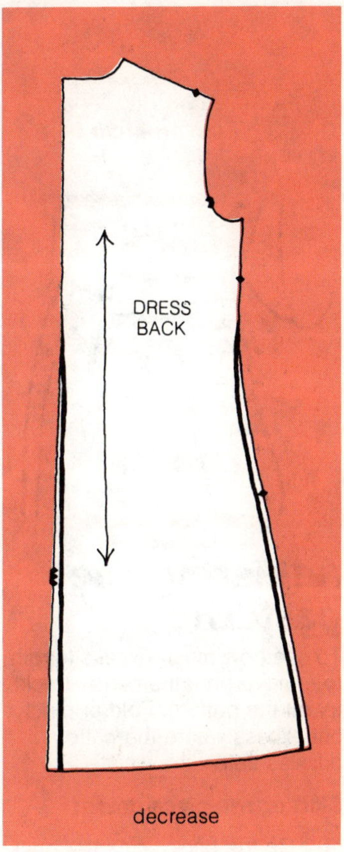

Fitting alert:

Wrinkles below the waist in back tell you that the garment is too long for you between the waist and hips at center back. It's a common problem that's easy to fix on the pattern or garment back.

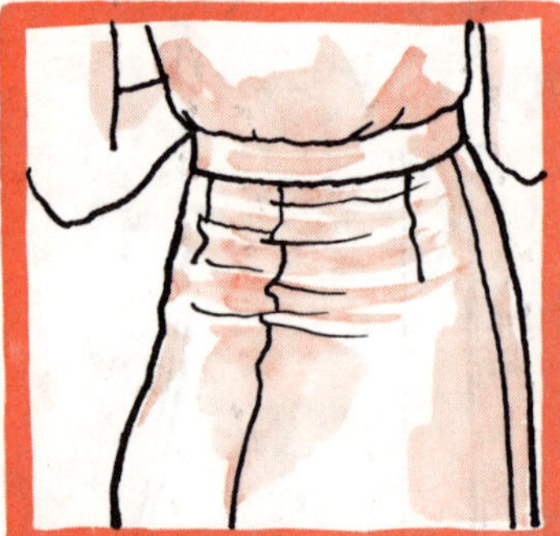

Adjusting the pattern

To see how much excess length to remove from the center back, try on the pattern. Fold or pinch out excess where the pattern buckles below the waist.

Skirt or two-piece dress:

1. On the back, at center back cutting line, mark down from the waist the amount needed.

2. Draw a new waist cutting line, tapering to the original one at side. The dart is now shorter and narrower. Widen the dart to restore original waistline.

Skirt with back yoke:

1. On the back yoke, at center back, mark down from the waist cutting line the amount needed. Redraw the waist cutting line, tapering back to the original at the side edge.

2. Mark in from side edge the amount needed to restore waist size. Redraw side cutting line, tapering to lower edge.

Fitting standard:

Clothes should fit smoothly over the seat—no bagging, pulling or wrinkling—and should allow you to sit comfortably.

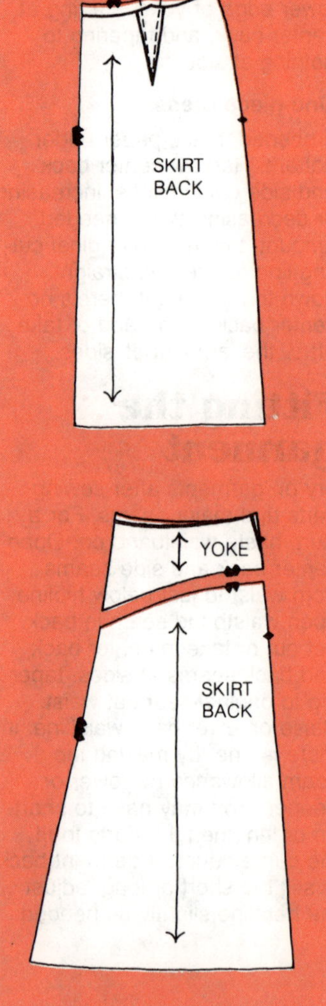

Make a practice garment

Because correct back fit is so important to really well fitting garments, you may want to make a "muslin" or practice garment. This way, you can test the fit of your pattern before you cut into any expensive fabric. A muslin can be made of any lightweight inexpensive fabric. Adding this simple step can assure you that your final garment will fit exactly the way you want it to, and give you a more professional look as well.

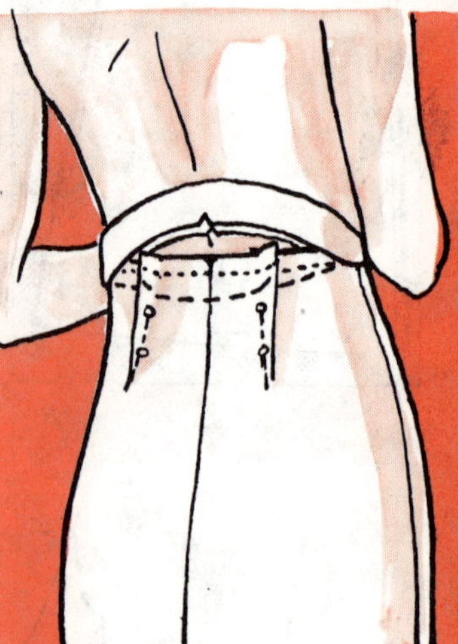

Fitting the garment

Try on the skirt or dress after you've sewn darts, yoke seams and vertical seams, and basted the waistline seam or the waistband in place. Open the waistline seam or remove the waistband in back. Remove excess length by making the back or back yoke waist seam allowance deeper at center back and tapering to the original waist seamline at the sides. Widen the darts enough to take up the extra width that you added to the waistline seam.

PANTS ADJUSTMENTS

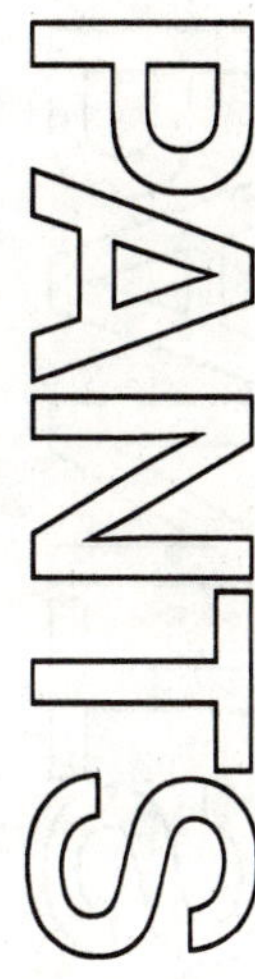

Most pants fitting problems require only one or two pattern adjustments. With our Fuss-Free methods, pants are easy to fit. First, select your correct pattern size. Then check the fitting standard here for pants, and follow the three steps on these pages for perfect fitting pants—measure, compare, adjust.

Fitting standard:

Pants should fit smoothly and comfortably with enough room to move, bend, or sit easily. Crotch depth and crotch length must be right, without any binding or sagging.

1. Measure

First, take the six body measurements on the chart below and write them in the YOURS column. To take correct body measurements, see the illustrations on pages 5-12. Next, add the minimum ease for woven fabrics (for stretchable knits, allow less ease) to the measurements indicated and record in the TOTAL column.

2. Compare

After you've filled in the PATTERN column, compare these measurements with those in the TOTAL column. If the total is more than the pattern, you'll need to add to the pattern; if less, you may need to make the pattern smaller. To help you decide whether to adjust, see pages 21-22. Then fill in the ADJUSTMENTS column.

PATTERN ADJUSTMENT CHART

	MEASUREMENTS				Adjustments (+ or −)
	Yours	Plus Minimum Ease*	Total	Pattern	
1. CROTCH DEPTH (seated on hard chair, from waist to chair seat)		¼ to ½" (6 mm to 1.3 cm)			
2. CROTCH LENGTH (from back waist to front waist through legs)		up to 1½" (3.8 cm)			
3. WAIST (around natural waistline)				(see pages 7-12)	
4. HIPS (same distance below natural waistline as on pages 7, 10, and 12)				(see pages 7-12)	
5. THIGH (around fullest part of leg)		2" (5 cm)			
6. PANTS LENGTH (from side waist to desired finished length)				(see envelope back)	

*for wovens; for stretchable knits, allow less ease

For waist and hip, fill in the pattern body measurements for your pattern size (see pages 7-12). For pants length, use the measurement on the pattern envelope back. For the rest, measure the pattern pieces as shown below, this page.

Most patterns have a printed crotch line; Simplicity Fuss-Free Fit™ patterns have printed lines for hip and crotch depth as well so you know where to measure. If your pattern doesn't have these lines, draw them in as shown (a). Draw hip and thigh lines at the same distance from waistline as you took your personal measurements. For crotch depth, draw a vertical line parallel to grainline from side waist to the crotch line.

Crotch depth: Measure the pattern at the Fuss-Free Fit™ line marked crotch depth or measure the one you've drawn (b).

If the natural waistline is above the pattern waistline seam, as on some trouser styles, first pin the waistband piece to the pants piece, matching seamlines. Then measure from the waistline marking or seamline down to the crotch line.

Some pants styles, such as hip-huggers, don't come all the way up to the natural waistline. To see how far down the upper edge of the pants are from the natural waist, compare the pattern pieces with a regular pants pattern or pair of pants. Be sure to match the pieces at the crotch line. Then, measure your pattern from the point above it where the natural waistline would be located.

Crotch length: Stand a tape measure on edge and measure from the waist seamline or waistline mark (see crotch depth, above), along the center front and center back seams to the crotch points. Don't include seam allowances. Add front and back measurements (c).

Thigh: Measure the front and back pieces at the thigh line between the seamlines. Then add the front and back measurements for thigh measurement (d).

3. Adjust

Make pattern adjustments in the order listed on the chart, since one adjustment may affect another adjustment.

Pro's tip:

If you'd like an easy way to take pants measurements, try this: Measure a pair that fits you really well. Lay them on a flat surface, measure the side length, crotch depth and crotch length. To get body measurements on woven fabrics, subtract 1½" (3.8 cm) from the crotch length, ½" (1.3 cm) from crotch depth. On knits, use the actual pants measurements.

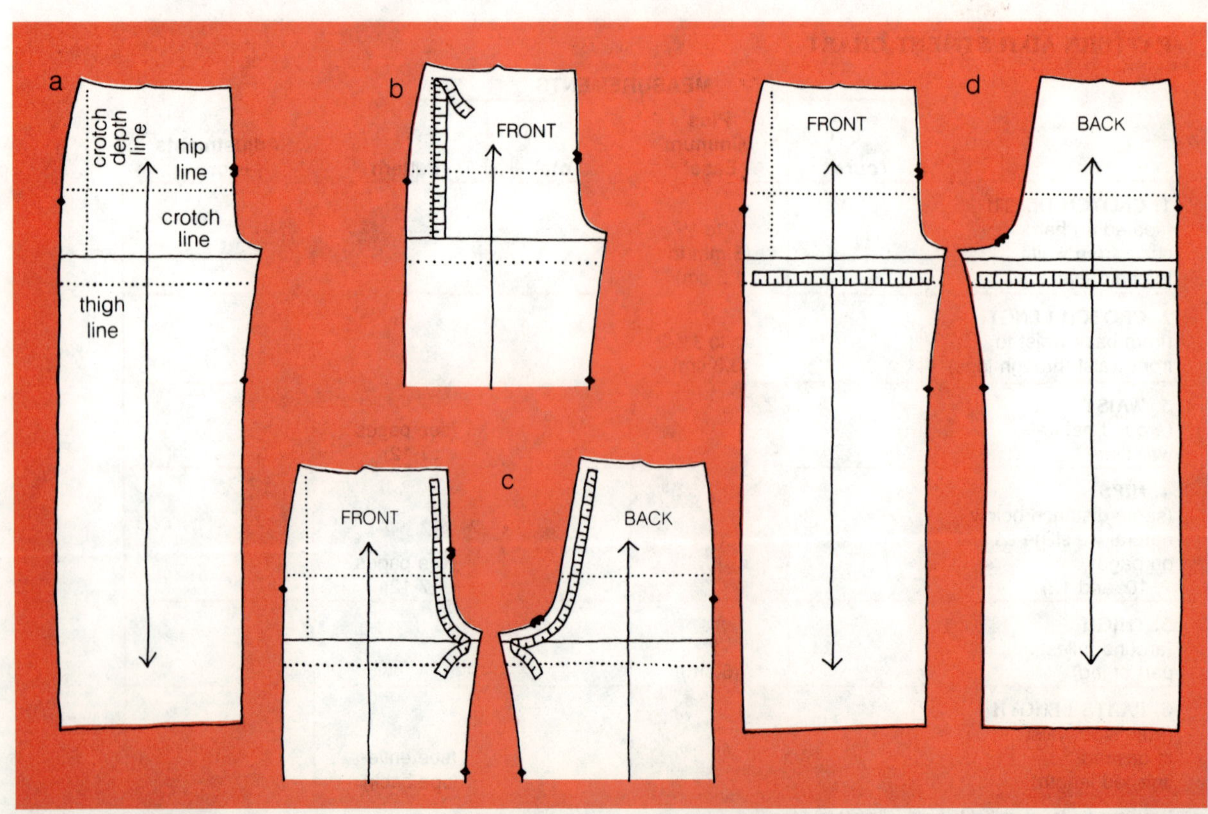

ADJUSTMENT BASICS

Crotch depth

Use the lengthen/shorten line above the crotch line on front and back for adjustments.

To shorten: Measure up from the lengthen/shorten line the amount to be shortened and draw a line parallel to it. Fold pattern on printed line and bring fold to the drawn line; pin. Correct cutting lines (a).

To lengthen: Cut pattern on lengthen/shorten line; spread it evenly the needed amount, keeping cut edges parallel. Place paper under cut edges; pin. Redraw cutting lines (a).

Remeasure crotch length after adjusting crotch depth.

Crotch length

You can divide the adjustment equally between the front and back, or add more to the back and less to the front, depending on your figure. For example, if you're round in front and flat in back, you may want to add to the front and shorten the back.

To shorten or lengthen: Stand tape measure on edge and measure the amount needed from center front waistline to where it meets crotch line; mark. To lengthen, extend crotch line out onto paper. Redraw crotch curve, tapering to original cutting lines (b). Repeat for back.

Note: To see if you need special adjustments, refer to pages 66-69. Since they affect crotch

length and depth, double-check these as well as overall length after making all the necessary special adjustments.

Waist, hip and thigh

First, see Circumference Adjustments, pages 28-29, for waist and hip. For thigh, measure in or out from both leg seams at thigh line $\frac{1}{4}$ the needed amount. Redraw cutting lines, tapering to original crotch point or hipline and extending straight down to hem edge (c).

Pants length

Adjust length on front and back as for crotch depth, left; use lengthen/shorten line on leg.

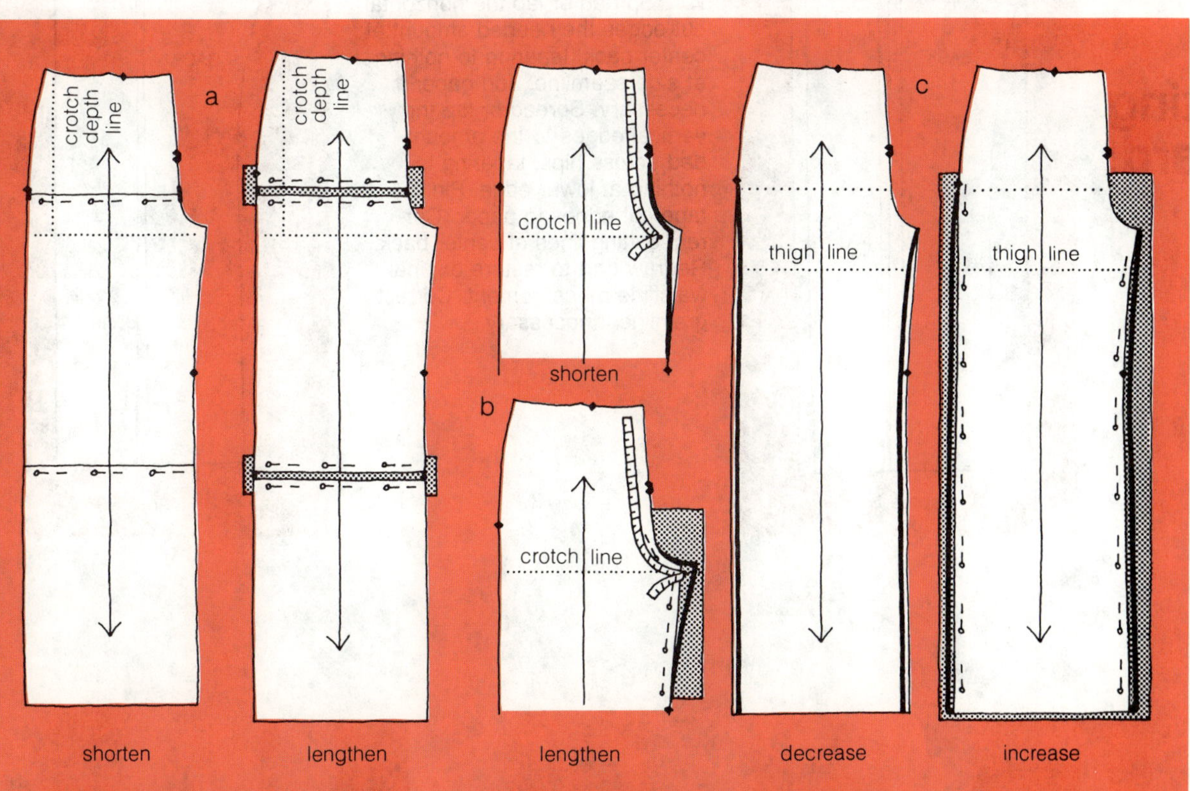

ROUND OR FLAT DERRIÈRE

Fitting alert:

If your pants pull across the derrière and the side seams pull toward the back, that's a sign that you need more room in back. If pants sag or bag in back, it's because there is too much length over the derrière. Either way, you can adjust the pattern to fit your body.

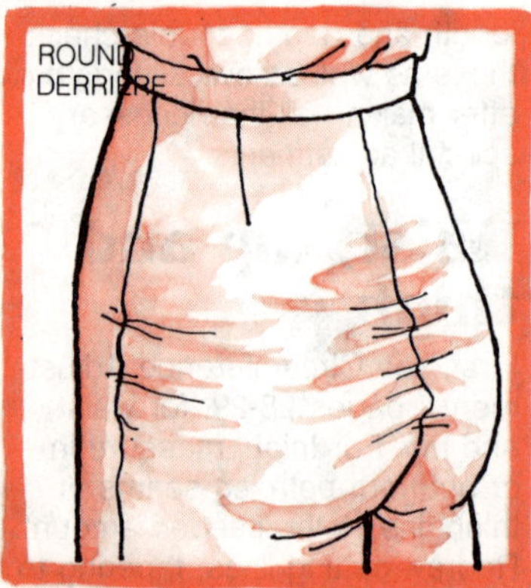

Adjusting the pattern

To decide how much you need to adjust: back pattern with iron-on interfacing or cloth. Then try it on, spreading it (cut pattern and pin to paper as described in Step 1, below) or pinching out extra fullness in length and width. Adjust the back only. Double-check the adjustment when trying on the pants.

Pants without yoke:

1. Draw a vertical line parallel to grainline through the center of the dart from waist to lower edge; draw a horizontal line just above the hipline, from center back to side edge. Cut the pattern apart on these lines.

2. Spread or lap the horizontal cut edges the needed amount at center back, tapering to nothing at side seamline; add paper if necessary. Spread or lap the vertical edges ½ the amount ded across hips, tapering to nothing at lower edge. Pin or tape cut edges to paper. Correct cutting lines at center back. Redraw dart to restore original waistline measurement. Correct grainline if necessary.

Fitting standard:

Pants should fit smoothly and comfortably with enough room to move, bend, or sit easily. Crotch depth and length must be right, without binding or sagging.

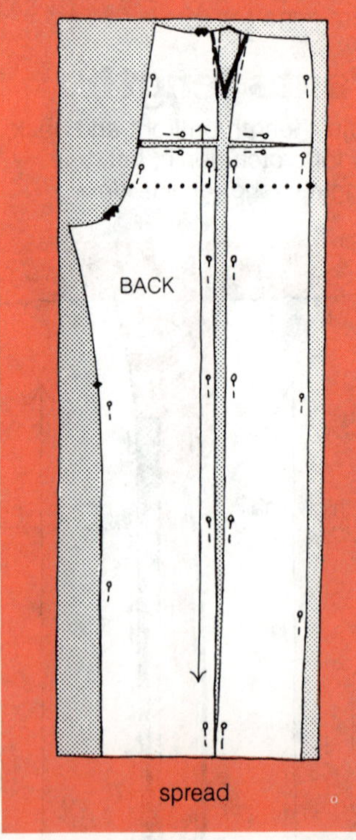

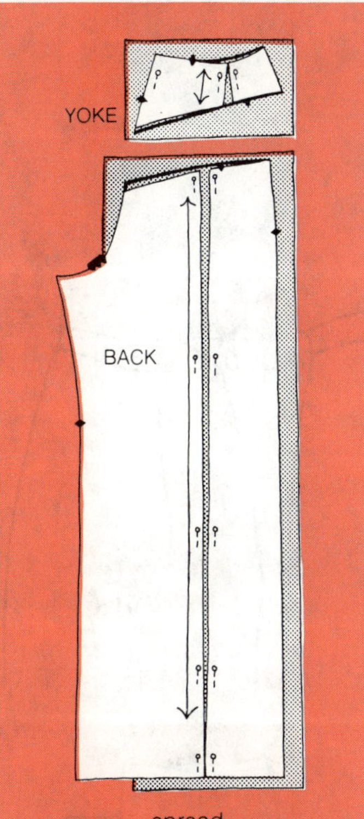

Pants with yoke:

1. Pin yoke and pants back pieces together. Draw a vertical line parallel to grainline through the middle of the pattern, from waist to hem. Separate the pieces and cut the pattern apart on these lines.

2. If needed, place paper under pattern. Spread or lap the yoke ½ the amount needed across hips at lower edge of vertical slash, tapering to nothing at waist seamline; spread or lap pants back the same amount, tapering to nothing at lower edge. At yoke seam, make both yoke and back seam allowances narrower or deeper ½ the amount needed at center back, tapering to original cutting lines at side edges. Pin or tape all edges to paper.

3. Correct all cutting lines.

Fitting the garment

Try on the pants after you've stitched the darts and basted the seams and waistband (or yoke sections) to pants.

To let out for round derrière, remove the waistband (or yoke) in back, open the side seams down to just below the hipline and open the center seam down to the notch. Then, let out the waistline or yoke seam, the back seam allowances of the side seams, and the center seam up to ⅜″ (1 cm).

For flat derrière, pin out any excess fullness at back seam allowances of side seams and at center back; then make the waistline of yoke seams deeper at center back. Shorten or lengthen the darts as needed.

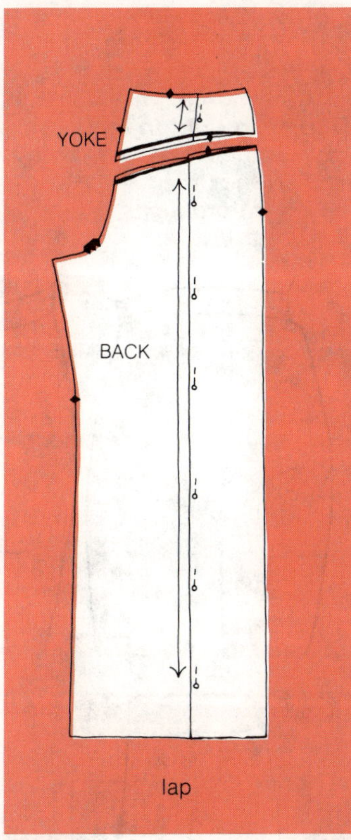

SMILE AND FROWN

Fitting alert:

Ready-made pants can give you a clue: If yours smile when you're standing, with wrinkles that point up from the crotch, they're too tight in the crotch area. If they frown, they're too loose in the crotch area. They may smile in front and frown in back, or the other way around, depending on your figure. To solve such problems, adjust the pattern and then make minor changes in fitting.

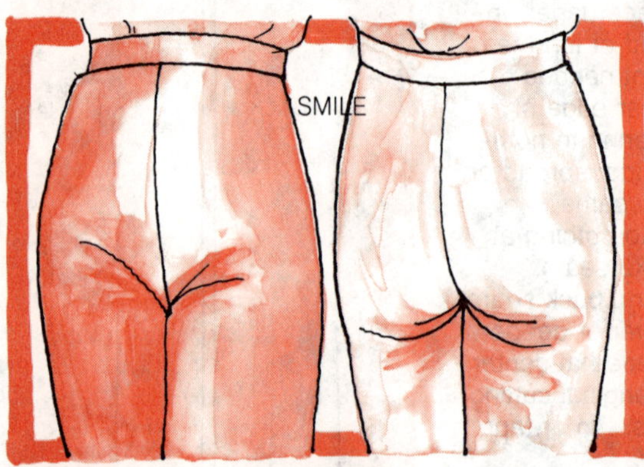

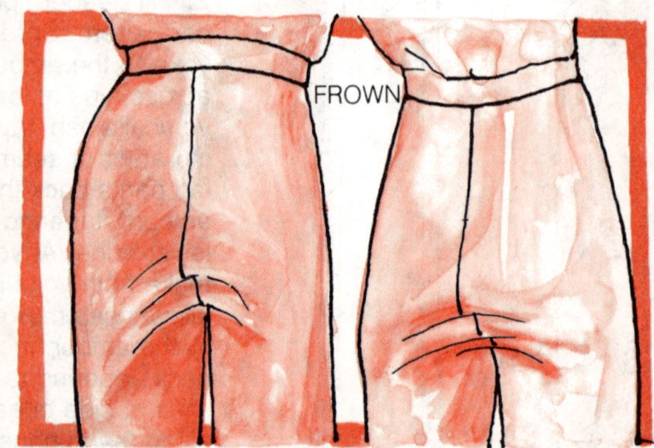

Fitting standard:

Pants should fit smoothly and comfortably with enough room to move, bend, or sit easily. Crotch depth and length must be right, without binding or sagging.

Adjusting the pattern

Smile or frown can be caused by the wrong crotch depth, crotch length or crotch curve. If crotch length or depth need adjusting see page 63 and adjust as shown here.

To change the shape of the curve, redraw it, putting the fullness where you need it, lower or higher than on the pattern or farther out or in. Remember, hollowing out a curve lengthens; filling in a curve shortens.

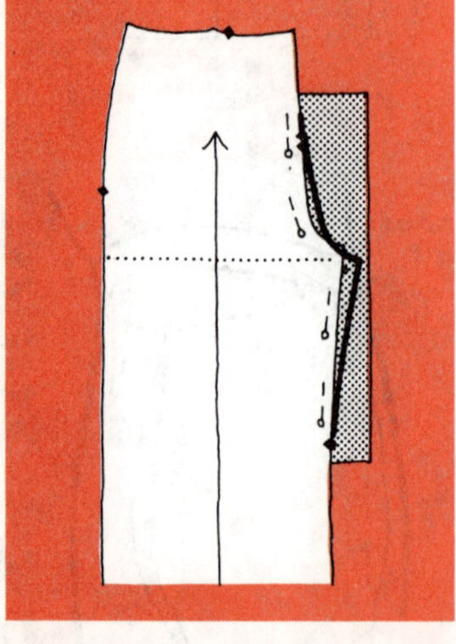

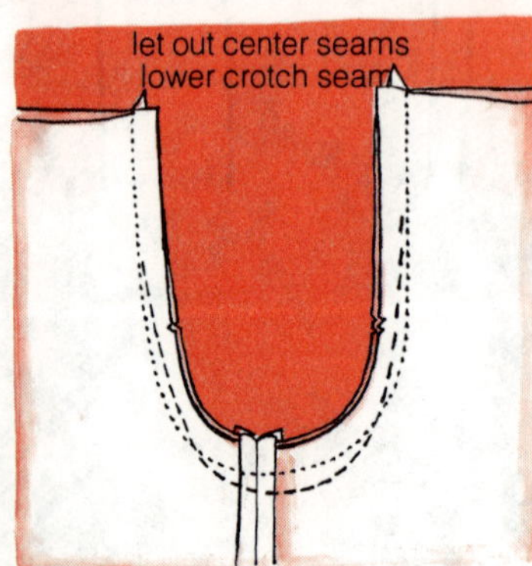

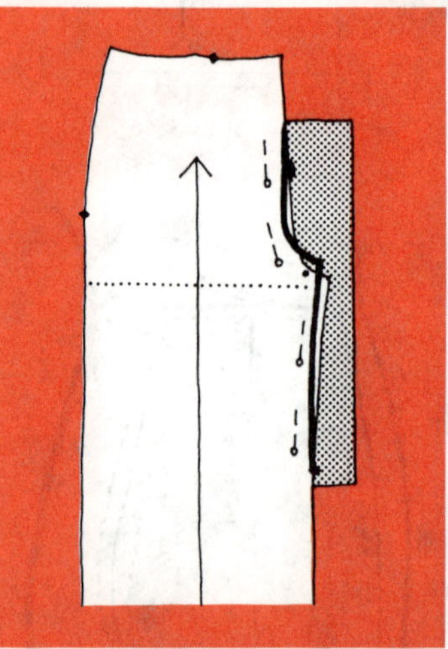

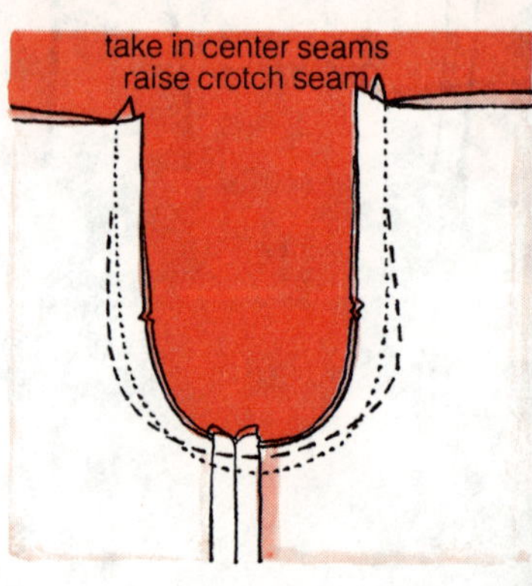

Fitting the garment

Try on pants after you've stitched the darts and basted the crotch seams and the waistband. If they still smile, remove waistband and let out waistline seam up to ⅜″ (1 cm). If necessary, widen crotch seam to make a deeper curve and let out center front and back seams up to ⅜″ (1 cm), tapering to original seamline below waist. If pants frown, take in waistline seam, let out crotch seam up to ⅜″ (1 cm), and take in the center front and back seams, tapering to original seam below the waist.

LARGE ABDOMEN

Fitting alert:

If your pants strain across the front below the waistline and the side seams pull toward the front, it means you need more room over the abdomen. You can adjust the pattern front to relieve the strain and give you a more comfortable fit.

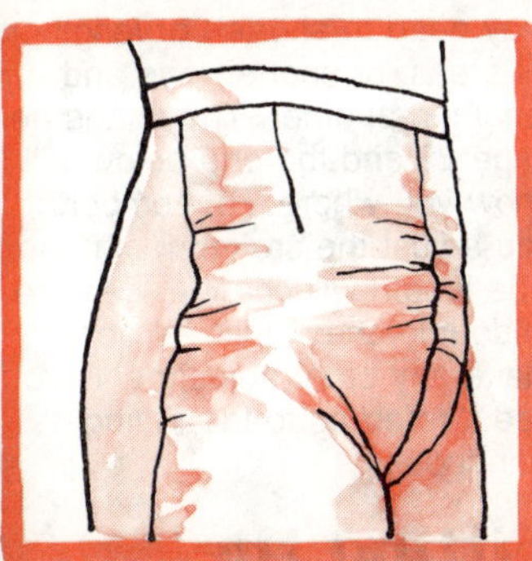

Adjusting the pattern

To see how much you need to adjust, first back the pattern with iron-on pattern cloth or interfacing (page 20); then slash the pattern and pin it to paper as described below. Try on pattern, spreading it as much as needed. Make the necessary adjustment on pattern front only.

1. Draw a line parallel to the grainline through the center of the dart from waist to lower edge. Draw a horizontal line between waist and hip from center front to side edge. Cut pattern apart on these lines.

2. Place paper under pattern. Spread horizontal cut edges the needed amount at center front, tapering to nothing at the side seamline. Then spread the vertical cut edges ½ the amount needed, tapering to nothing at hemline of lower edge. Pin or tape all edges to paper.

3. Connect the cutting lines at center front. Redraw the dart, keeping it the same length as the original one and making it wide enough to maintain the original waistline measurement.

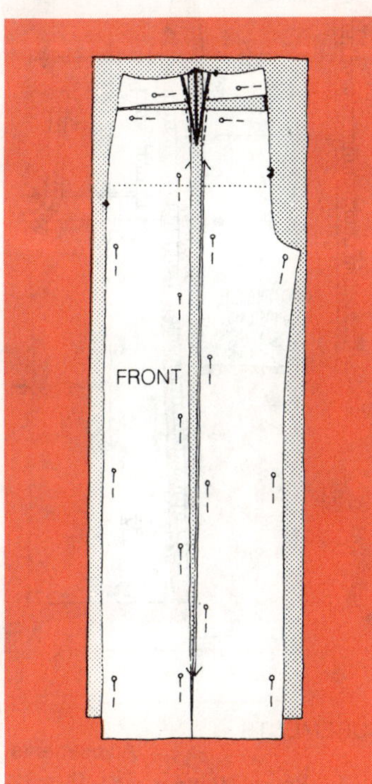

Make a practice garment

It's really worth the little extra time it takes to make a "muslin" or practice garment to assure well-fitting pants. After you have adjusted the pattern, make a muslin out of lightweight, inexpensive fabric. Then, make any fine fitting adjustments you need before you cut into the fashion fabric. The end result will be a perfect fitting pair of pants with a professional look.

Fitting the garment

Try on the pants after you've stitched the darts and basted the seams and the waistband. Remove the waistband in front, open the side seams from the waist down to the hipline and open the center front seam down to the notch. Let out the waistline seam, the front seam allowances of the side seams, and the center seam up to ⅜" (1 cm), tapering all new seamlines to original at waistline. You may also need to shorten front darts slightly to fit the curve of the abdomen.

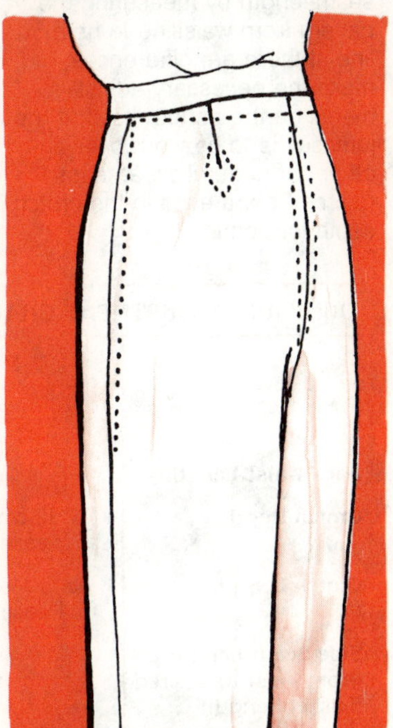

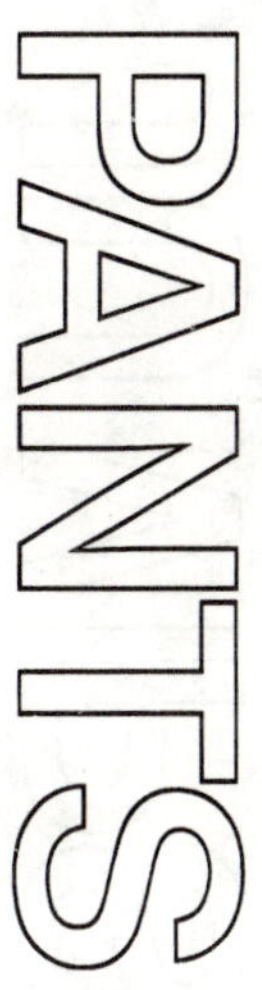

JUMPSUITS

A jumpsuit is a combination of bodice and pants, with or without a waistline seam. Use adjustment and fitting methods that apply to both areas.

Select a pattern

Start with the correct pattern size, using bust or chest measurements as your guide. Then measure, compare and adjust the pattern before you cut out your fashion.

Take the measurements

The most important measurements for fitting jumpsuits are the back waist length, crotch depth and length, and the side seam length. Record your measurements (see pages 6-12 and 63) on the chart below, adding or subtracting ease where you need it. Then fill in the pattern measurements, using the pattern envelope back for the back waist length. Measure the pattern as directed on pages 63-64 for the crotch depth and length. Take the side seam length by measuring the pattern from waistline to hemline. If there are differences, make the necessary adjustments on the pattern itself. If the jumpsuit is to be worn over another garment, allow at least 1″ (2.5 cm) extra ease in the crotch depth for comfort.

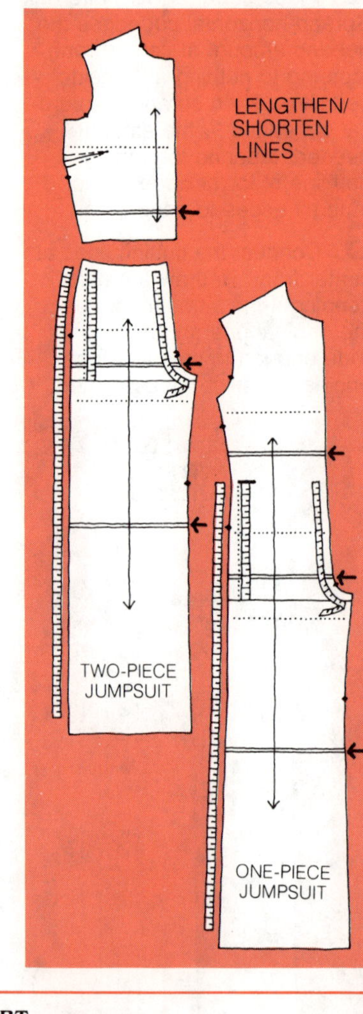

Adjusting the pattern

Lengthen or shorten the pattern where needed in the bodice, crotch, or leg areas. For how-to's, see pages 27 and 65. You may need to shorten or lengthen all areas, or shorten one and lengthen another. The charts on page 22 and the one below will show you where. Remember, if you adjust the crotch depth, the side length will change. Be sure to double-check that as well. Make any other adjustments you need, referring to the Fitting Handbook.

Fitting the garment

Try on the jumpsuit after you've stitched the darts, shoulder and side seams and basted any seams you're unsure of. If there is no waistline seam, you can lengthen the body of the jumpsuit by taking a deeper seam at the crotch curve, or you can shorten it up to ⅜″ (1 cm) by taking a narrower seam. If there is a waistline seam, adjust the length and/or crotch depth there. For special adjustments, see the Handbook, pages 30-69.

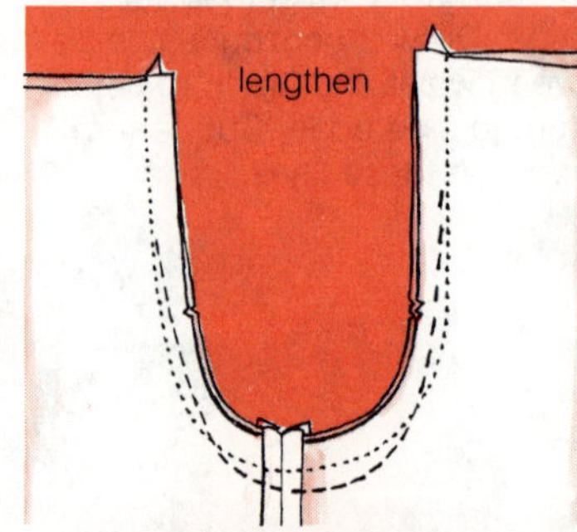

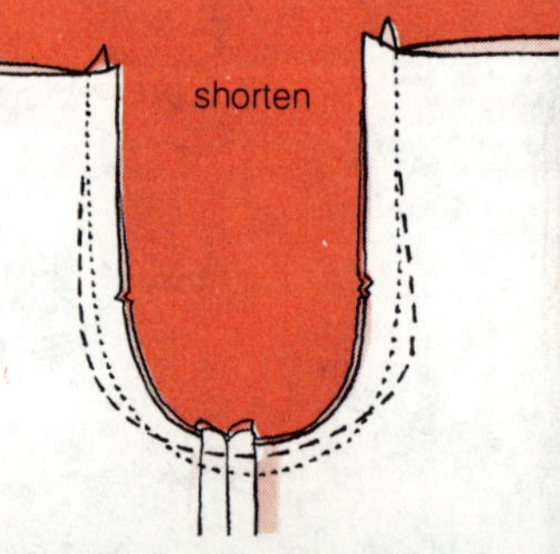

JUMPSUIT ADJUSTMENT CHART			
	MEASUREMENTS		Adjustments (+ or −)
	Yours	Pattern	
Back Waist Length			
Crotch Depth	+ ¾″ (2 cm) ease		
Crotch Length	+ up to 1½″ (3.8 cm) ease		
Side Seam Length (from waist to desired finished length)			

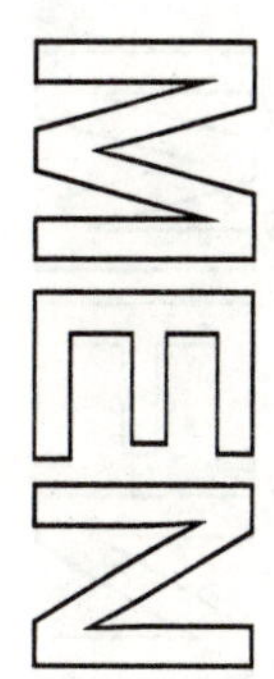

FITTING MEN'S CLOTHES

The techniques for fitting men's clothes follow the same basic Fuss-Free methods for all clothing. Measure, compare and adjust is the successful three-part formula for perfect fitting fashions for men. Before you begin, refer to pages 9–10, how to take measurements and choose pattern sizes. In this section, we focus on fitting jackets and pants. For adjustments on other types of garments, see the Handbook for special adjustments.

JACKETS

Fitting a suit or sport jacket the Fuss-Free way takes three simple steps:

1. Taking body measurements accurately.

2. Comparing them with pattern measurements (see the chart on page 22).

3. Adjusting the pattern.

Simple pattern adjustments

Minor changes in length and circumference are easy to do, by lapping or spreading the pattern on the lengthen/shorten lines as shown here.

Length adjustments

See the instructions on page 27 to shorten or lengthen the pattern pieces at the printed lengthen/shorten lines. Be sure to make the same matching adjustment on all three corresponding jacket body pieces, both sleeve pieces and any adjoining facings that are to be stitched to these pieces (a). If there are separate pattern pieces for the lining, adjust them the same way. After adjusting the length, be sure to check the markings for buttonholes and pockets. Reposition these, if necessary, to maintain the correct proportions of the jacket or suit design.

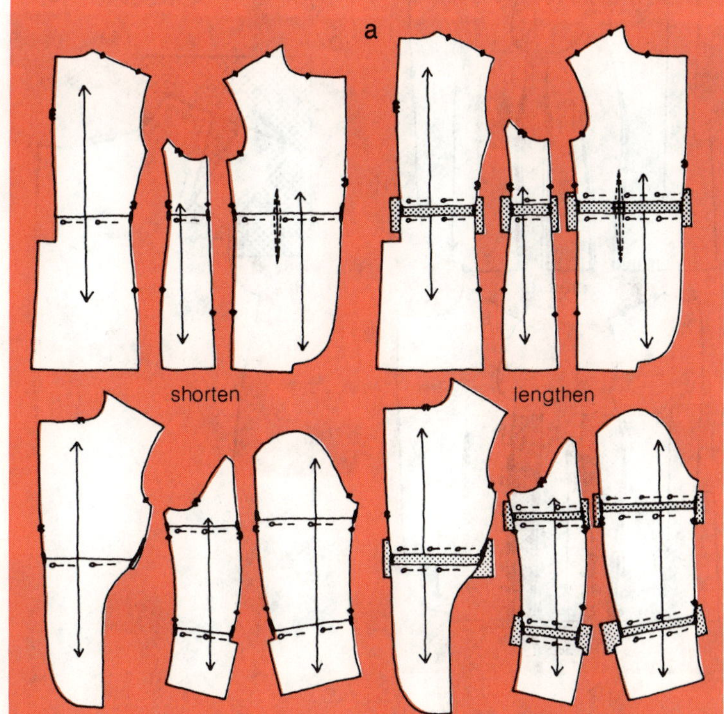

Fitting standard:

Jacket is balanced well on the body with a smoothly fitting upper back. Shoulders follow natural body lines and are padded to give a symmetrical appearance. Waist tapers slightly to natural waistline. Sleeves hang straight and even; collar hugs the back of the neck and does not gape. Lapels roll smoothly down to jacket closing, lie close to the body.

Circumference adjustments

Since jacket patterns are chosen by chest size, they should not require changes in that area. Circumference changes can be made, however, at the waist and hip.

Large hips and/or waist make a jacket ride up and places a strain on the seams and buttonholes. Small hips and/or waist make the jacket too large and cause lengthwise folds.

Decide on the total adjustment that is necessary and divide by 8. If the adjustment is 1″ (2.5 cm) or less for large waist or hips, do not alter the pattern. Let out the seam allowances instead. Otherwise, decide on the total adjustment that is necessary up to 2″ (5 cm) and divide by 8. (You'll be changing 4 seams and 8 seam allowances.) Increase or decrease this amount at the side seam allowances as shown (a), tapering to the original cutting lines 3–4″ (7.6–10 cm) above the waistline. For example, 2″ (5 cm) divided by 8 equals ¼″ (6 mm) at each seam allowance. Do not alter the center back seam. Be sure to reposition the pockets and buttonholes, if necessary, after the pin-fitted garment has been tried on.

Special Adjustments

The most common special adjustments on a jacket are for shoulders, back and sleeve.

SHOULDERS

Broad shoulders make the jacket pull in the back, sleeves and across the chest. Shoulder length is too short.

To adjust the pattern, cut apart the pattern of both back and front pieces. Place paper under pattern. Spread the amount needed. Pin or tape cut edges in place; correct seamlines (b).

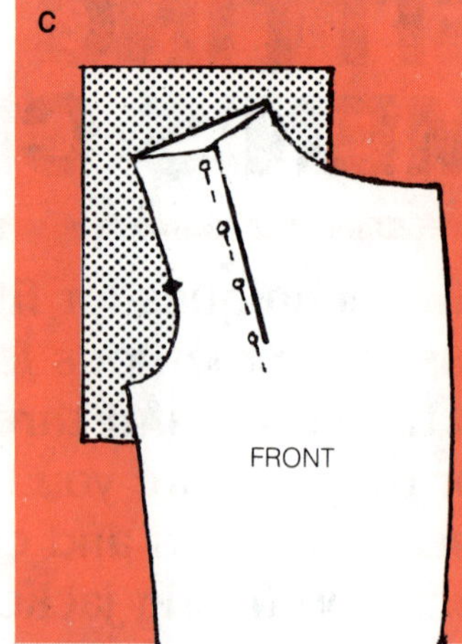

Narrow shoulders cause a too-long shoulder length and make the armholes fall below the shoulder point.

To adjust the pattern, cut the front and back pattern pieces as shown for broad shoulders (b) but lap ½ the amount needed. Pin or tape in place; adjust the seamline (c).

Square shoulders can cause the armhole to be too short at the shoulder point, and form wrinkles below the collar.

To adjust the pattern, place paper under pattern. Raise the shoulder point the amount needed on both front and back pattern pieces and make a new seamline (d), tapering to the original seamline at the neck edge. Pin or tape in place. Adjust armhole seamlines on front and side pieces to correspond.

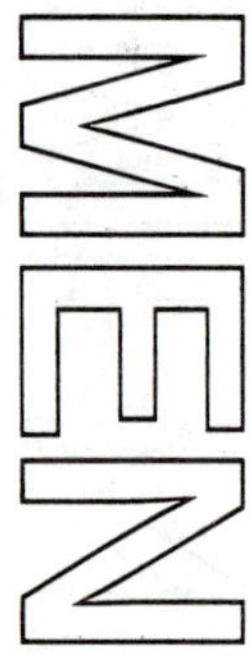

Fitting standard:

Jacket is balanced well on the body with a smoothly fitting upper back. Shoulders follow natural body lines and are padded to give a symmetrical appearance. Waist tapers slightly to natural waistline. Sleeves hang straight and even; collar hugs the back of the neck and does not gape. Lapels roll smoothly down to jacket closing, lie close to the body.

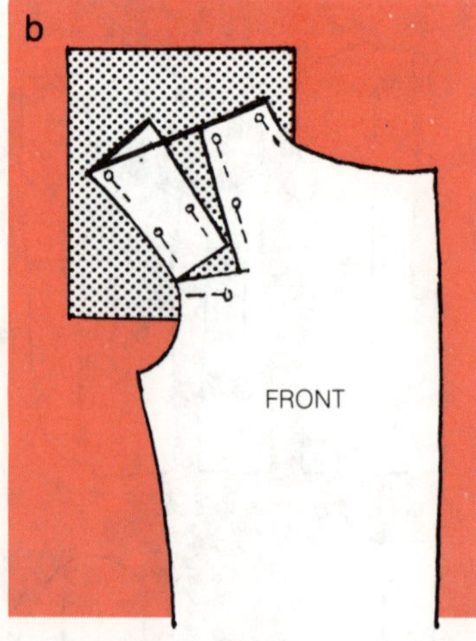

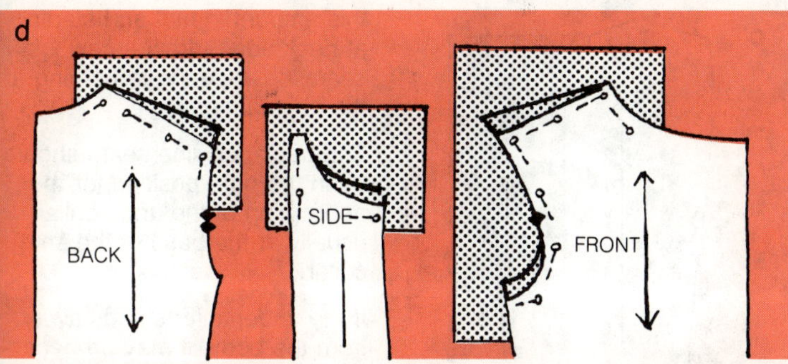

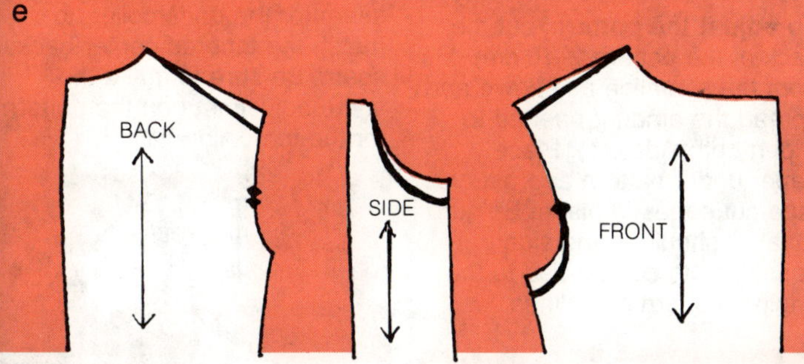

Sloping shoulders cause extra length at the shoulder point and create diagonal wrinkles above and below the armhole.

To adjust the pattern, lower the seamline and shoulder point on both pattern back and front pieces (e), tapering to original seamline at neck edge. Adjust armhole seamlines on front and side pieces to correspond.

Shoulder Pads: If a man has sloping or narrow shoulders, adjust the pattern accordingly. Then, when you fit the jacket, use shoulder pads as a finishing touch. Fit the jacket with sleeves sewn in and the armhole seam pressed open above the notches and trimmed (f). Pin the shoulder pads to determine the best position—usually one-third toward the front and two-thirds toward the back, with pad extending ⅜″ (1 cm) beyond armhole seam (g). Loosely tack pad to shoulder and armhole seam.

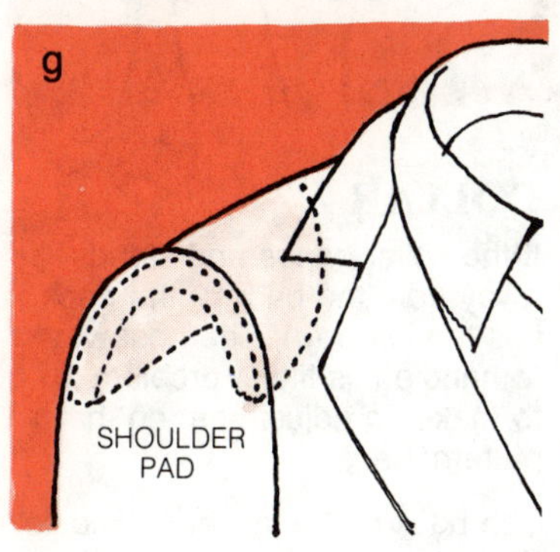

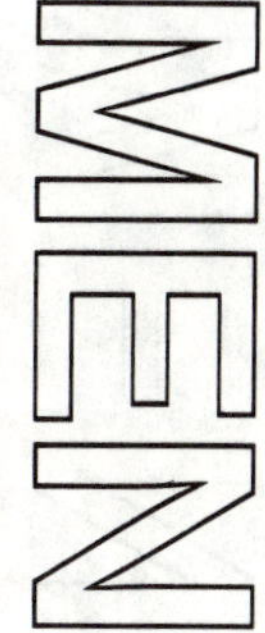

BACK

Round back makes the back of the jacket pull up and stand out. The jacket front swings open, away from the body. The length of the jacket upper back must be increased (h).

Adjusting the pattern: Draw a line on the pattern back 4″ (10 cm) below the neckline from the center back almost to the armhole. Cut pattern apart. Place paper under pattern and spread the amount needed. Tape or pin cut edges in place. Correct the center back seamline (i).

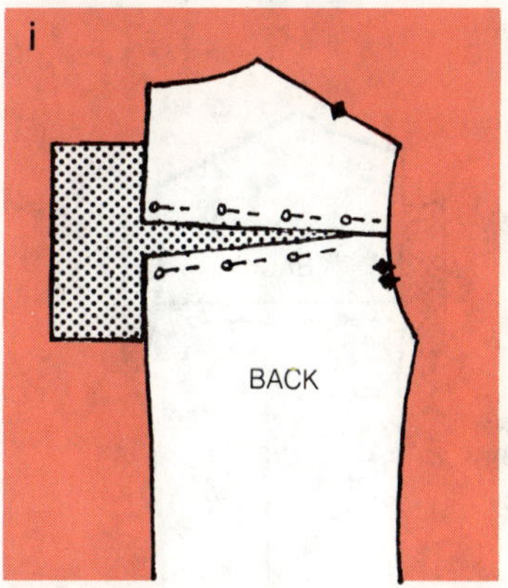

An **erect back** makes the back of the jacket sag. The fronts of the jacket will cross each other. The length of the jacket upper back must be decreased (a).

Adjusting the pattern: Cut the pattern back as for round shoulders 4″ (10 cm) below the neckline from the center back close to the armhole. Overlap ½ the amount needed (b). Tape or pin cut edges in place. Correct the center back seamline.

A **wide back** makes the jacket too tight across the shoulders and under the armholes.

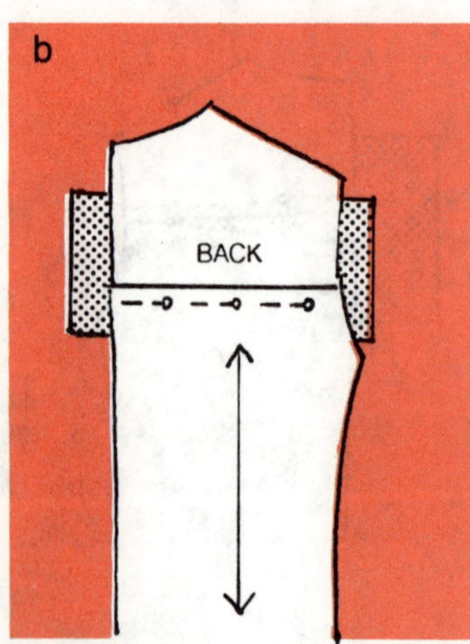

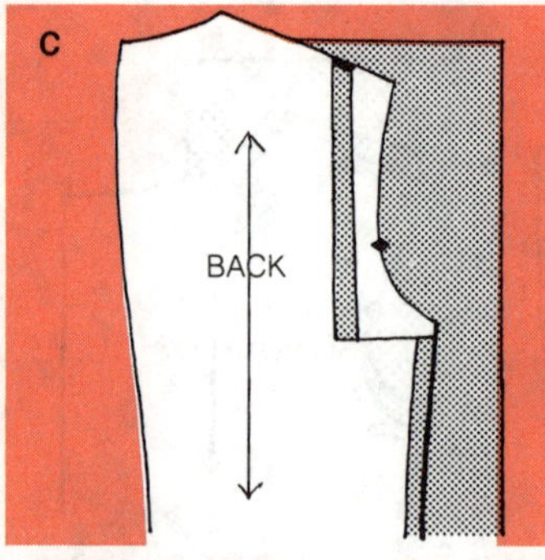

To adjust the pattern, cut the back of the pattern 2″ (5 cm) from the seamline as shown and spread the amount needed to widen both sides (c). Place paper under pattern and pin or tape cut edges in place. Be sure to taper shoulder and side seamlines to correspond to the original pattern seamlines.

COLLAR

If the collar gapes and stands away from the back of the neck, it is too large (d). The best way to handle this fitting problem is to make an adjustment on the pattern pieces.

The back of the jacket should lie flat against the body just below the neckline. If there is any gaping, adjust the pattern as follows:

Measure the amount that needs to be taken in on the jacket back so that it lies flat. Divide this amount in half and starting at neck edge, draw a new seamline, tapering to nothing at the original seamline.

The back neckline seam should be in the right position for the application of the undercollar, usually at the base of the shirt collar.

If the undercollar stands away from the body, it may be necessary to cut a deeper center back seam for the undercollar, to match the tapered center back seam. Be sure to make the same adjustment on the pattern for the top collar.

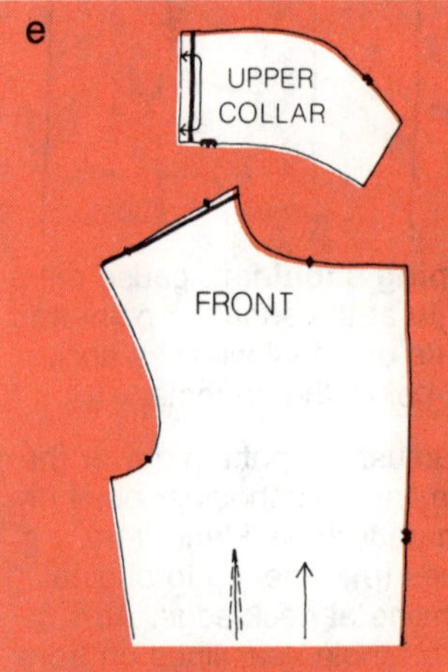

If there is wrinkling or bulging below the undercollar, that means there is excess length in the center back neckline seam. Measure the amount that needs to be removed and draw a new seamline (e). Baste undercollar to jacket and check the fit.

SLEEVES

If sleeves are too short or too long, follow the instructions for lengthen/shorten on page 27.

When sleeves are too narrow or too wide, follow the instructions for width adjustments on page 27.

PANTS

Simple Adjustments

To see if crotch depth, crotch length, hip and thigh width and finished length need adjusting, see pages 63-65. For waist adjustments, see page 74. Be sure to read the special hints below before measuring.

Waistline location: The location of the waistline affects crotch depth, crotch length and finished side length measurements. On regular pants the top of the waistband rests at the natural waistline.

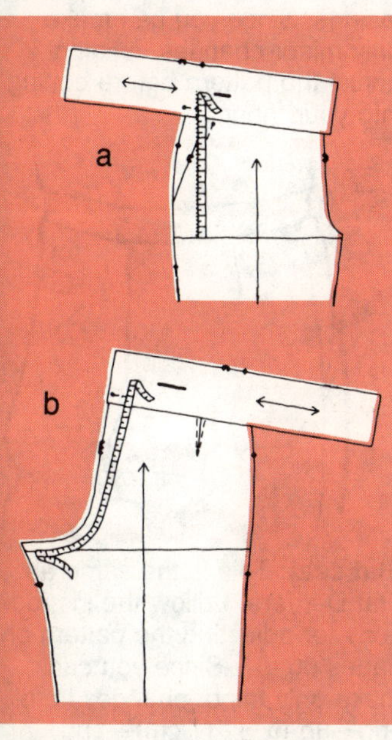

To measure crotch depth (a) and crotch length (b) on a regular pattern, pin waistband to pants piece, matching seamlines. Then measure from waistline mark on waistband.

Some pants, like jeans, ride low on the hips, with the top of the waistband 1 or 2″ (2.5 or 5 cm) below the natural waist; the illustration on the pattern envelope will give you a clue. To see

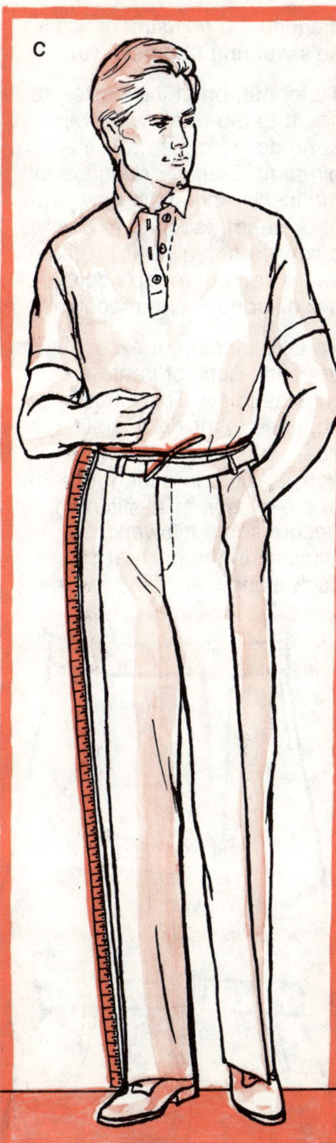

how far down the waistband will be, compare the pattern with a pair of ready-made regular pants OR compare finished side length (on back of pattern envelope) with the finished side length of a regular pants pattern. Then take the body measurements and pattern measurements from that point (c). Pin any yoke or pocket pieces to the pants pattern before measuring (d).

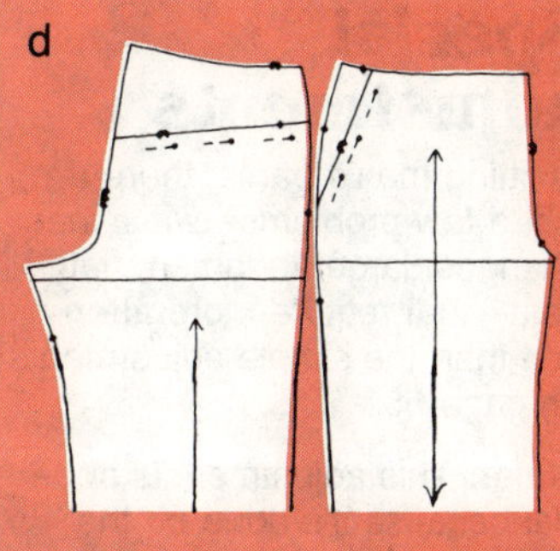

Pants length: The finished hem should just touch the shoes in front, without breaking, and should come to the top of the shoe heel in back. This usually means that the hem slants from front to back, with the back a little longer than the front (e). Mark and finish the hem after you've completed the pants and have fitted them in other areas. The hemming stitches should be hidden between the layers of fabric to avoid being caught on the heel of a shoe. You may have to slash hem allowance vertically for an inch (2.5 cm) or so at front crease area to allow for slant of hem. A slight tuck will form in hem allowance at the back crease area for the same reason.

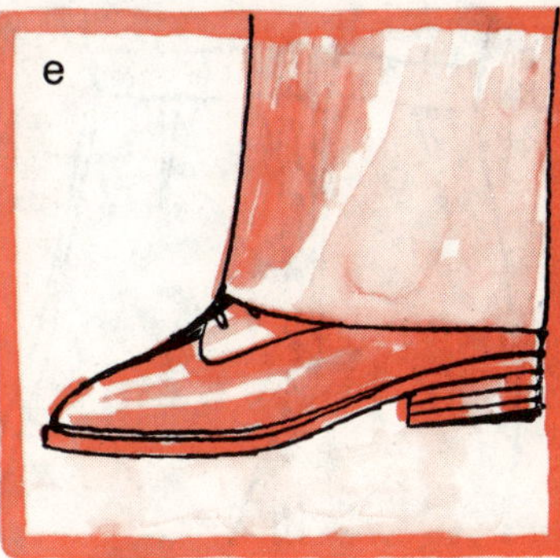

Fitting standard:

Pants should fit smoothly and comfortably with enough room to move, bend or sit. Crotch depth and length must be right, without any binding or sagging.

Special adjustments

In fitting men's pants, there are just a few problems—waistline changes, large abdomen, flat seat—that require more attention than the simple adjustments on page 65.

Waist: This adjustment is special because it's done on the garment rather than the pattern. It's very easy to make a fitting change at the waist on men's pants because the pants and the waistband have an extra-wide center back seam allowance. So if a man has a habit of alternately gaining and losing weight, you can let out or take in the center back seam by marking the adjustment while he's wearing the pants (a).

To let out, open the center back seam of the pants and waistband down to the hipline and re-pin to fit. Transfer changes to the inside and stitch new center back seam, tapering to original seamline at hipline (b). Press seam open, turn top edges under diagonally and machine-tack.

To take in, pin out excess width at center back of pants and waistband (c). Then transfer changes to inside and stitch new seam (d). Finish as above. If you've taken in a lot, trim some of the excess after stitching. Secure seam allowances by stitching in the ditch at center back along waistband seam (e).

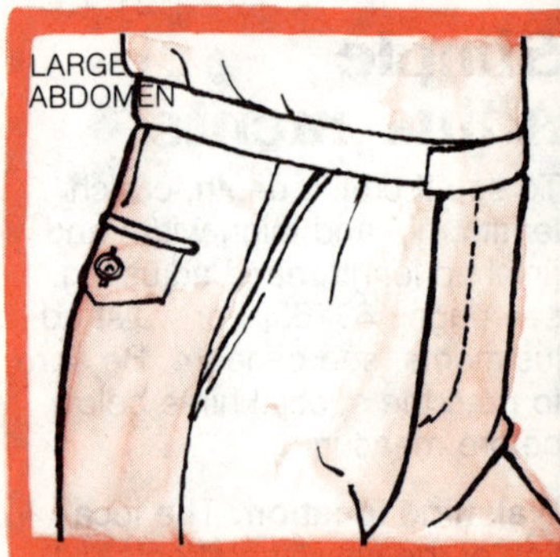

Large abdomen: For pattern adjustments and fitting, see page 69. When you adjust the pattern front, be sure to adjust the fly, front pockets and pocket facings. Since you can make only minor changes in fitting, adjust the pattern before cutting into your fabric.

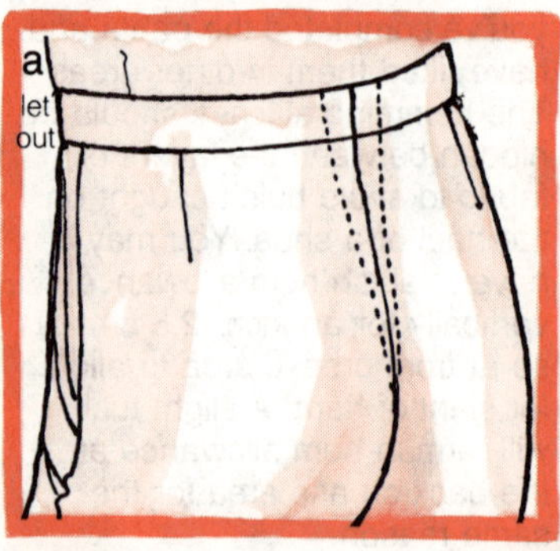

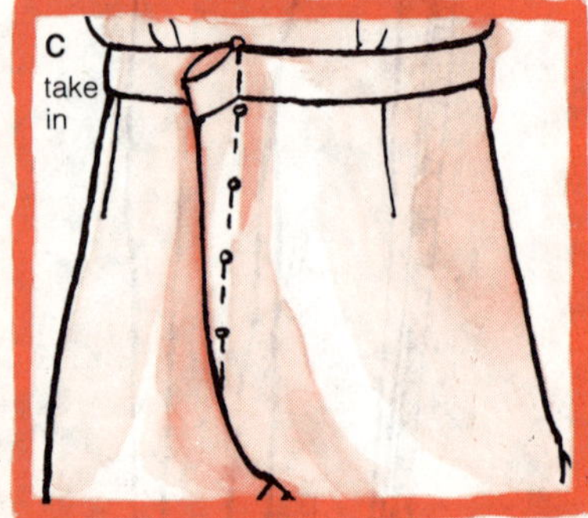

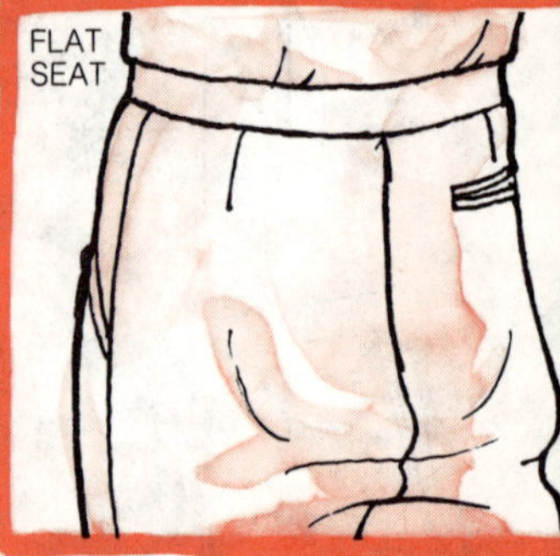

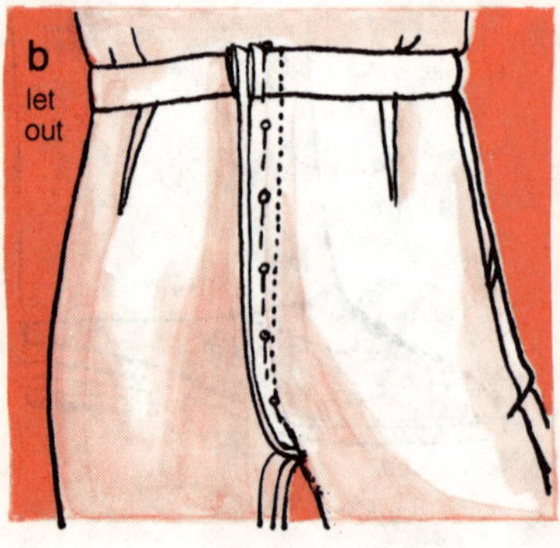

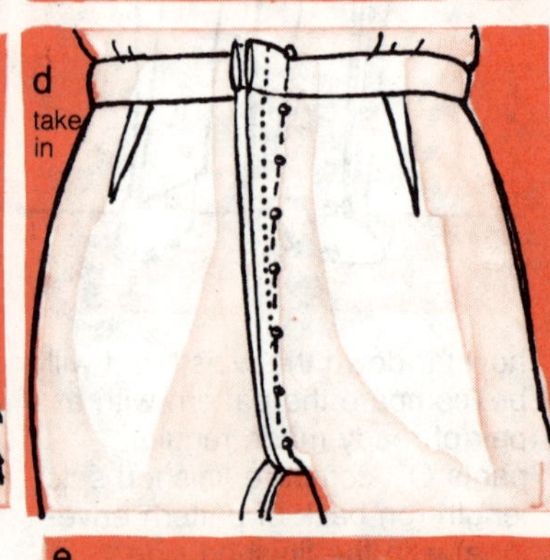

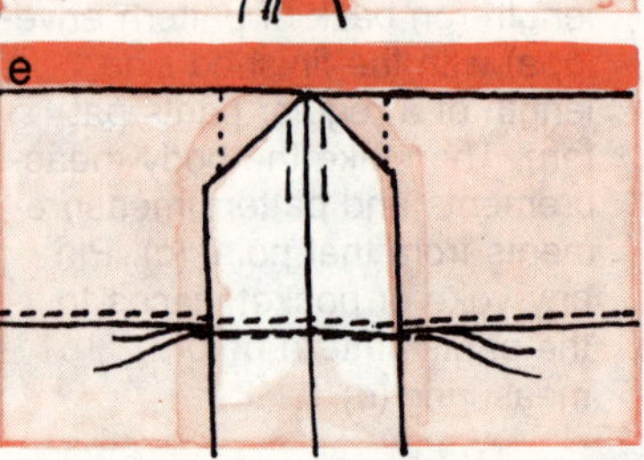

Flat seat: This is the same as Flat Derrière. Follow the instructions for adjusting the pattern on pages 66-67. Since you can make only minor changes in fitting—up to ⅜" (1 cm)—and they're usually time-consuming to do, you should adjust the pattern before you cut out the pants

FITTING CHILDREN'S CLOTHES

Most children's clothing relies on simple straight lines that hang from the shoulder. See pages 11-12 to take children's measurements accurately. Choose the correct size by circumference or width measurements, rather than by length. Length adjustments are simple to do after the child's pattern size has been established.

Adjusting the pattern

Most patterns for children are simple in style and require little or no adjusting—perhaps a length adjustment or two. You can lengthen or shorten a fairly straight pattern at the hemline; for other length adjustments, draw shorten/lengthen lines on the pattern perpendicular to grainlines at locations shown (a). Or refer to the general shorten or lengthen how-to's on page 27 for more help.

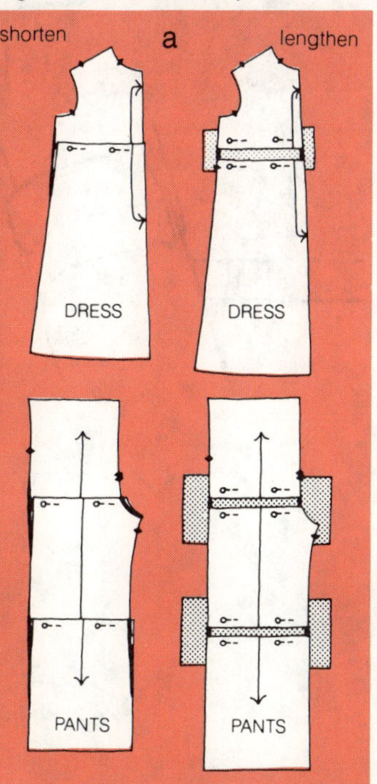

Fitting standard:

Fitting children's clothing is not usually a problem, because their clothes are loose. But it is important that their clothes fit them correctly through the shoulders and that lengths are right for both comfort and safety.

CHILDREN

Fitting standard:

Fitting children's clothing is not usually a problem, because their clothes are loose. But it is important that their clothes fit them correctly through the shoulders and that lengths are right for both comfort and safety.

Growth allowances

Probably the most important consideration in sewing for children is the growth factor. Because children grow so fast, adding growth allowances to the clothes you sew makes them last longer and does not affect their fit at all.

Two ways to build in growth allowances to children's clothes are by adding tucks or inserting elastic at strategic points.

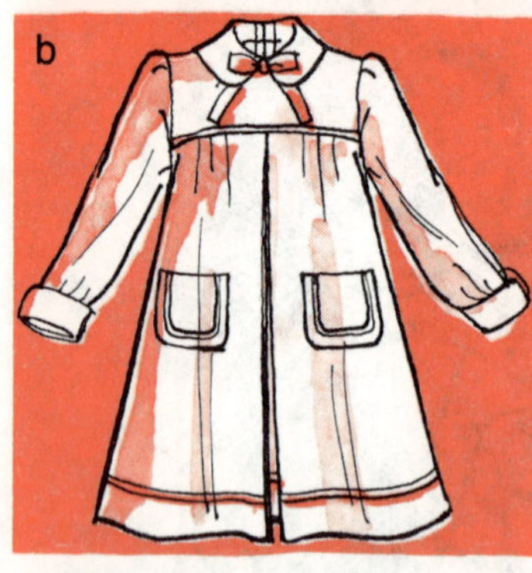

GROWTH TUCKS

The most obvious place to allow for a child's growth in height is the skirt hem. At straight hemlines you can add 3″ (7.6 cm) to the hem allowance, depending on the style of the garment and the size of the child. Form a 1½″ (3.8 cm) tuck in the hem allowance; baste and press toward the hemline. Finish the hem (a). To release the tuck later, remove the basting and press a new hemline. Stitch trim or ribbon over the old hem crease if necessary (b).

On a dress with a waist seam, cut front and back bodices 1-3″ (2.5-7.6 cm) longer than the pattern, extending the side seams straight down. Baste a tuck half as wide at the waistline on the inside; press it up. Join bodice to skirt (c). When tuck is released, remove the lower part of the zipper and restitch it. Cover any fade marks with a contrasting ribbon or sash (d).

For long or short sleeve shirts, blouses and pants for both boys and girls: add as much as 3″ (7.6 cm) to the hem allowance on clothes with a straight hem. Then baste a 1½″ (3.8 cm) tuck within the hem allowance and press the tuck down. Sew the hem as usual. When the extra length is needed, release the tuck by removing the basting stitches. Press the new hemline and cover the old one with trim or stitching if necessary.

STURDY SEAMS

Children's clothes will last longer and stand up better under normal stress if you sew them with these sturdy types of seams.

Flat-felled seams are good for straight seams on clothes like playwear and dresses. With wrong sides together, stitch a plain seam. Press to one side. Trim the underneath seam allowance to ⅛″ (3 mm). Turn top seam allowance under ¼″ (6 mm) and pin or baste it over the trimmed edge. Topstitch close to the fold (e).

Topstitched seams can be used almost anywhere and are decorative as well as serviceable. Stitch a plain seam; press it to one side. Then, on the outside, topstitch ⅛ to ¼″ (3 to 6 mm) from the seam through all layers (f). Or, after stitching, press seam open and topstitch ⅛ to ¼″ (3 to 6 mm) on each side of the seam as shown.

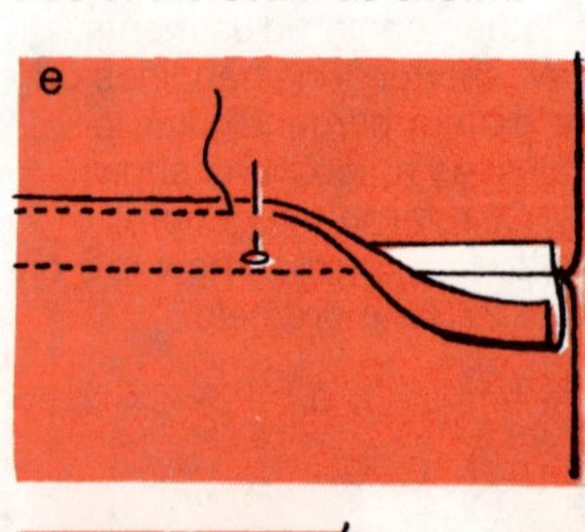

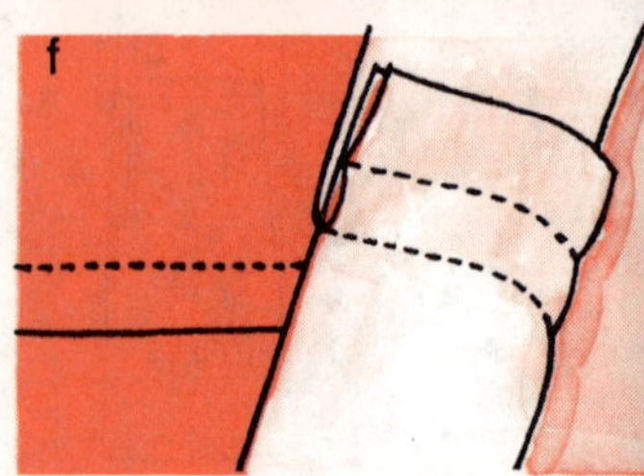

ELASTIC INSERTS

For children who grow quickly in width as well as in height, elastic is a problem solver. Up to 1″ (2.5 cm) of extra ease can be added to a pattern with elastic inserts.

On a dress with a waistline seam, add ½″ (1.3 cm) at the side waist edges of the bodice back and skirt back patterns, tapering to the original cutting lines. Sew the dress, omitting back darts and zipper. Sew bias tape casing along back waist seam. Insert elastic 1″ (2.5 cm) longer than the child's back waistline measurement, catching the ends in the side seams (g). If there is a zipper in back, cut elastic and tape in half and place ends at center back. Stitch across ends. Insert zipper and stitch in place (h).

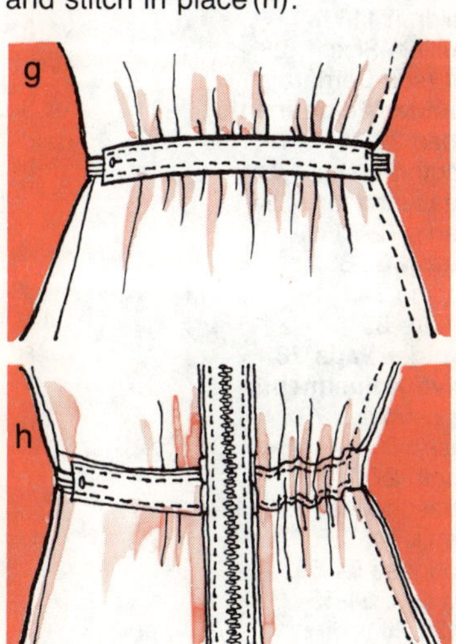

On skirts and pants with waistband, add ½″ (1.3 cm) to each side of back at waist and waistband. Sew notched edge of waistband to waistline. Use elastic ¼″ (6 mm) narrower than finished band; cut it the length of the child's back waistline. Zigzag elastic to inside of back waistband, stretching it to fit (i). Secure ends; sew waistband (j).

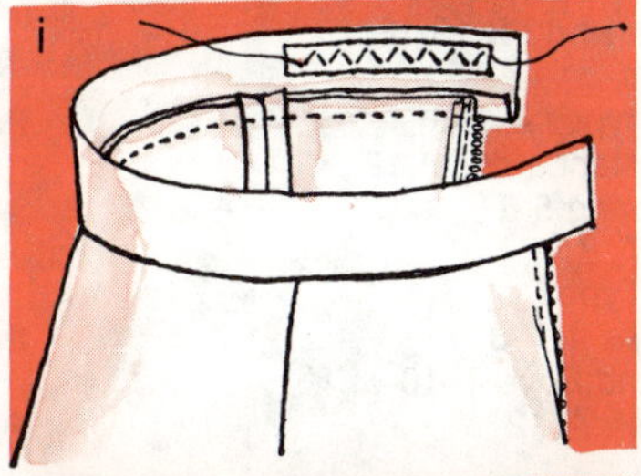

Adjusting for Chubbies

Chubbie patterns are available for girls who weigh more than the average for their age and their height.

If the style you want does not come in Chubbie sizes and is loosely fitted, it may not need any adjustments. For fitted styles, buy the size by chest and waist, then adjust the length. Or, choose the size by back waist length and add width, using the slash and spread method (k). Cut front, back and sleeve pattern sections apart as shown. Spread front, back and sleeve pieces ¼ the needed amount.

Pin cut edges to paper and redraw the cutting lines. Adjust any pieces to be stitched to the bodice to match changes.

To enlarge a neckline, draw a lower cutting line on front and back pieces. Make the same adjustment on all the facings and/or collar pieces so they correspond to the neckline (l).

INDEX